The Classical Seat

A GUIDE FOR THE EVERYDAY RIDER

BY SYLVIA LOCH

HORSE & RIDER

First published in Great Britain in 1988.
Reprinted in 1991, 1994, 1996 and 1998.
© Sylvia Loch, 1988.

Horse & Rider Magazine,
D. J. Murphy (Publishers) Ltd,
Haslemere House,
Lower Street,
Haslemere, Surrey GU27 2PE

ISBN 0-9513707-1-5

Printed in the UK by
Falder Matthews Limited
Seax Way, Southfields Ind. Park
Basildon, Essex SS15 6SW

Contents

ACKNOWLEDGEMENTS

There are many people to whom I am grateful for helping constructively in the writing of this book.

Firstly, my thanks to Lucinda Green who was the first person to read the original articles and the first person to endorse the book. Lucinda's own books have enjoyed worldwide success, yet she has always found the time to encourage others in the same field in a most stimulating and generous way. Having ridden at my late husband's establishment in Suffolk, she was able to appreciate the importance of the use of the seat in preparation for dressage as well as the advantage of riding schoolmasters.

Secondly, I shall always be very grateful for the encouragement given by Geoffrey Gibson as I researched the subject of the seat. As a Master Saddler and classical horseman, his special knowledge of saddlery and posture were invaluable and he was most generous with his time and advice.

I have also been much helped in discovering the fundamental points of the classical seat by riding in one of Mr. A. J. Foster's dressage saddles for over a decade. Although designed for the modern world, saddles such as these, built on Portuguese classical lines, help the rider in to a more balanced position. This is not so with all conventional (dressage) saddles.

On the medical side, I am indebted to John Gorman whose own books on the subject of human posture, particularly relating to back pain, have been most helpful. I also wish to thank the senior physiotherapists at Walnuttree Hospital in Suffolk, particularly Susan Millar; similarly physiotherapists David Wilson and Tony Brightwell. Their assistance and encouragement gave me great confidence particularly when I was told that if more riders adopted the classical seat, they would have to treat far fewer patients.

On the Continent, I particularly wish to acknowledge the riders of the Portuguese School of Equestrian Art, who, together with their *chef d'equipe*, Dr. Guilherme Borba have been an inspiration. As a pupil of equitation in Portugal for so many years, I have come to understand the tremendous quality of stillness and lightness which is the hallmark of the true classical horseman. I owe the horsemen of the Iberian Peninsula a great debt as did my late husband, Henry, who was probably the only English cavalry officer to be totally accepted as a genuine *cavaleiro* at the great horse festivals of those countries.

It would be impossible to list the names of the great writers of history and the modern day whose books have made such an impression on me. However, if I were to advise a pupil embarking on the path of classical equitation to take but three books away on a desert island, I would suggest *The Training of Horse and Rider* by Podhajsky, *The Spanish Riding School* by Hans Handler, and *Reflections on Equestrian Art* by Nuno Oliveira: one practical, one which demonstrates all the colour and search for perfection embodied in riding's Age of Splendour, and one inspirational. These three books, although different from each other, are bonded together with purist ideals of light, harmony and artistry.

Finally, my deep thanks to Kate O'Sullivan and Steve Humfress at *Horse and Rider* for believing so much in this book and for making it a most rewarding one to write.

To Richard

My non-horsy but perceptively brilliant lawyer husband whose clear, unprejudiced eye for balance has helped me time and time again to write with clarity and conviction. In understanding the huge debt I owe all the horses I have had the privilege to ride over so many years, he has generously welcomed my own two Lusitanos, Andorinha and Palomo, to our home in Suffolk with open arms.

Why Another Book?

There are so many excellent books on the market relating to dressage. We are advised about training both horse and rider from day one to the highest level. We are taught the aids for each movement, simple to advanced. There are endless books on preparing the horse for competition and others which define competition technique as well as nursing the reader through the tests. We learn what the judges are looking for and how to please the judges, and so on and so forth.

When I was first invited by Kate O'Sullivan at *Horse and Rider* Magazine to write a series on the classical seat, it occurred to me that there was no simple guide which concentrated one hundred per cent on teaching the rider not only how to sit but how to *feel* what he is sitting on. This puzzled me, for over many years of learning and later teaching and still learning today, I know that a rider who has mastered the classical seat and by feel has progressed to the stage of using his seat effectively, holds in his hands the key to the art of riding.

Riding classically encourages all that is natural, noble and beautiful in the horse.

THE USE OF THE SEAT

Why therefore, I wondered, had more not been written on the seat itself? I knew that if the seat was right, everything else would fall so much more easily into place. Thus riding dressage could become relatively natural and more of a feeling activity than one bound up in complicated rules and regulations.

Yet teaching the use of the seat has little or no place in the preparation of students for riding examinations in Britain. Even at Fellowship level thinking on the subject is often hazy. Those few ideas on the subject which are voiced are more often than not at variance and some of the ideas put forward are so complicated that the ordinary rider is immediately discouraged. "Dressage? Oh, that's not for me!" is an all too familiar sentiment. With such a lack of understanding, it seems odd that so few have attempted to put down in writing some basic principles which would make dressage attractive, comprehensive and natural whilst at the same time corresponding to the ideals of the world's great classical masters.

Nowadays, many instructors tend to concentrate all their energy into training the horse – whilst the rider comes a distant second. This seems totally back to front. To quote Charles de Kunffy who was a member of the Hungarian Olympic Team and who is now based in California: "The horse knows how to be a horse if we will only leave him alone . . . but the riders don't know how to ride. What we should be doing is creating riders and that takes care of the horse immediately."

On the Continent the first priority is to produce good riders who are capable of schooling horses up to a high standard.

The English style of riding changed dramatically with the growth of hunting. Many people were no longer interested in the finer points of equitation and were quite content to be passengers.

This of course has a snowball effect in that the well-schooled horses so produced will help new novice riders to reach high standards who will in turn be able to school their horses. Therefore there is a constant supply of highly schooled horses.

The main reason this happens less in Britain is because hitherto we have been far more interested in hunting, racing and jumping than in the art of equitation. Provided that there has always been a steady stream of willing, hotblood horses which enjoy being up in front whilst riding out across country, there is often little enthusiasm for the study of the finer points of schooling. It is rather a case of sit tight, kick on and go!

Because of this, saddles have largely evolved to complement a forward-going, cross-country seat, rather than a classical seat. Only in comparatively recent times have some riders turned to a more centrally designed dressage saddle, but even the most up-to-date versions often leave much to be desired. If we are to excel at dressage however, it is vital to start off with suitable accoutrements. Our young riders should be encouraged to sit as we mean them to go on but this does call for equipping them with better saddles. Such a move would pay dividends as it becomes increasingly plain that a good grounding in dressage is highly beneficial to the overall performance of the horse generally. This has been proved time and time again by the success of people like Virginia Leng, Bruce Davidson and Mark Todd whose excellent preparation of the horse in dressage has led to more agility and control in the jumping phases of eventing.

The series of articles which I wrote for *Horse and Rider* which first appeared in the summer of 1985 was aimed exclusively at improving the rider on the flat, i.e.

preparing him for dressage and for controlled and safer riding. I hoped to woo the average rider who had always felt dressage was stilted and far beyond him. I felt strongly that if one could teach people to sit correctly and to strive for a classical position right from the onset of training so they actually felt they were aiming for something that was natural, noble and beautiful, there was a chance we could produce a chink of light through the mists which still for all too many enfold the subject of dressage in this country.

People should be taught to aim for the ultimate. It must be wrong to start someone off in one particular way; and then only when they pass a certain grade, may they be allowed to share the secrets of a higher echelon. In the words of John Donne, "Aim for the stars and you might yet touch the moon."

CLASSICAL RIDING

Classical riding should be open to everybody who is interested in improving their own and their horse's performance. There has always been far too much mystique wrapped round the subject of dressage. The time has come to unwrap those dark folds and bring everything out into the sunshine. After all dressage is nothing more than teaching the horse to be a pleasant, safe and controlled ride.

To encourage those people who have always thought dressage was beyond them, I have attempted in this book to throw a new emphasis on the subject – simply to think of riding correctly not as something artificial and contrary to their natural instincts but rather something so logical that they may wonder why they never thought of it before in that obvious way.

It is my firm belief that if we adhere to Nature's basic laws of gravity and locomotion and transfer some of the feelings we experience on the ground into our riding, we shall start off on the right track. By encouraging the rider to throw away the rule-book and think naturally – i.e. in terms of what feels most comfortable for his body – then body awareness and finally body control will be developed. This is vital to the student of equitation, for riding is so very much a feeling activity – two live creatures striving to understand each other and to feel comfortable and confident

one with the other.

It was the Greeks who first developed classical horsemanship as we shall read in the next chapter. The principles laid down by Xenophon are still remarkably relevant today. But classical riding reached its height in Europe in the 17th and 18th centuries inspired by the cultural reverberations of the Renaissance. What has been handed down to us by the great Masters of equitation of the time has provided a very solid basis for riding. All these principles have been based on natural laws, and from thereon were honed and refined by countless dedicated horsemen over the ages. It is perhaps not enough to talk about the art of classical riding, but also of the science. Put together harmoniously the end result should be beautiful.

Of course one cannot learn to ride correctly merely from reading a book. In a lifetime of learning, one will never know all the answers. Riding is so much a matter of feeling, not only with the body but with the mind and spirit. No one can teach us to feel except the horse and our own physical realisation. Intellectual awareness of what our bodies are doing at a given time and in a given situation may take years to develop. Such feeling is a gift that comes more easily to some than to others. However, with perseverance and concentration, this awareness can be acquired and heightened. Emotionally, we must really want to become classical riders, which means nothing more than being at one with the horse. Our love for the horse and our desire to acquire the beauty which is the end result of helping him to be happy and balanced under us should equip us to strive towards perfection. Humility will be learned, but confidence and suppleness will grow.

Deliberately, my book has been kept simple. It will not teach you humility, or feeling, or convert a body which has never experienced athleticism in any form into an overnight gymnast.

My aim is to encourage people to become aware of their own capabilities. All too many people feel that dressage is beyond them and holds no real promise for them and their horses. By encouraging people to consider equitation in a less formidable light through a greater understanding of the simple mechanics of

the human frame, I hope to give them a starting point for classical riding. For those who are already on that path, I hope this book will encourage useful discussion with their tutors. If it helps to smooth away some of the constrictions, the worries and the misunderstandings that have existed in the past and which have clouded the whole spectrum of equitation, then I shall be well satisfied.

Classical riding reached its height in Europe in the 17th and 18th centuries. The Portuguese Royal Master of the Horse, the Marquis of Marialva (above), was a follower of La Guerinière. His methods are still vigorously followed by the Portuguese and Spanish equestrian academies of today.

The Classical Seat
HOW IT AROSE

Over two thousand years ago in ancient Greece, Xenophon[1] wrote: "I do not approve of a seat which is as though the man were on a chair, but rather as though he were standing upright with his legs apart."

These fundamental words sum up all the theory behind the explanations in this book. Wherever possible throughout these pages I have included simple examples to illustrate how we may best achieve Xenophon's principles. These will relate particularly to a layman's study of the human frame and how it is built to cope with not only its own athletic movement but also that of the horse underneath. There is nothing new or revolutionary about these teaching methods save that they are kept purposely simple. When instructing a rider on horseback, I refuse to lose sight of what he would naturally be able to do on the ground. This is what I mean by the classical seat as opposed to the dressage seat. There are many different dressage seats, depending upon the interpretation of the instructor, but only one classical seat.

The term 'classical' relating to art or to sport indicates that which the ancient philosophers of Athens and Rome deemed the most logical. It maintained the ideal balance between the laws of nature and the mind and body and was closest to beauty and harmony. In art this implied sculpture or painting of a lifelike nature; with regard to horsemanship, it implied a style which did not go against nature. Most of us have read enough about primitive man to realise that we were not created to spend our lives sitting at a desk or in an armchair. *Homo sapiens* was never intended to be *homo sedens*[2] (sitting man). Rather we were equipped with the type of spine which enabled supreme mobility from an upright position, i.e. standing, running or jumping. It is very important to remember this when you ride.

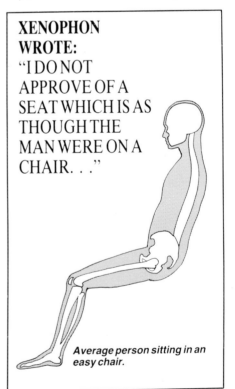

XENOPHON WROTE: "I DO NOT APPROVE OF A SEAT WHICH IS AS THOUGH THE MAN WERE ON A CHAIR. . ."

Average person sitting in an easy chair.

[1] Xenophon (approx. 445-355 BC) the Athenian philosopher and cavalry leader wrote a famous treatise on equitation *Hippike* which has been translated into almost every language in the world and is still regarded as applicable today in its principles as it was over 2000 years ago.
[2] *Homo Sedens* – is the title of a book concerned with posture and lumbar problems by John Gorman MA which can be ordered from: John Gorman, Oaklands, New Mill Lane, Eversley, Basingstoke, Hants RG27 0RA. It costs £4.95.

THE NEED FOR GOOD POSTURE

Despite the fact that many people in the western world have become sedentary creatures, we have not regressed so far down the evolutionary scale that we cannot revert to good athletic posture. In fact our spines have not changed at all in the last one hundred thousand years or more and have to be treated properly. Riding classically therefore can bring about a greater awareness of treating our bodies with respect. This has helped people with backache, and those who in the past moved about sloppily and were likely candidates for back pain in later life. Increasing popularity of the Alexander Technique* is a good example of how the public are becoming more aware of the importance of posture. Its principles complement both riders and non-riders, and with regard to the former are very similar to those of classical riding.

Riding in the classical manner therefore will not only improve performance in the saddle. It will also increase mobility and versatility in our everyday lives.

From now on let us forget about sitting chairlike in the saddle and begin to picture the rider in a more perpendicular position, as Xenophon says "as though he were standing upright with his legs apart." This is what is meant by the classical seat. Its hallmark is a proud, deep uprightness. You do not have to be a rider to recognise this. Every non-equestrian visitor to the Spanish Riding School of Vienna will remark on the very special seat of the riders.

A SAFE AND CONTROLLED SEAT

Not only is the classical seat a safer seat, it is a controlled seat. It enables the horse to become balanced and light, and able to execute the movements required of him by the rider. It may be put to advantage not

---

* Anyone wishing further information about the Alexander Technique should write to The Society of Teachers of the Alexander Technique. 3b. Albert Court. Prince Consort Rd.,London. S.W.7.

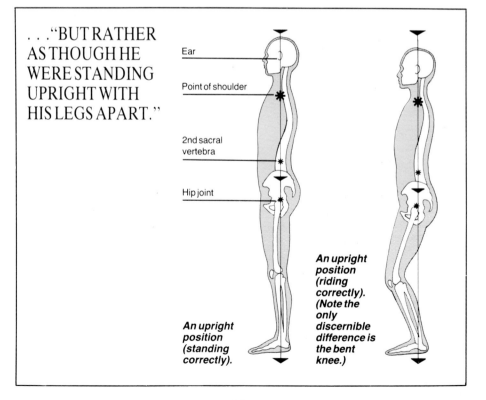

. . ."BUT RATHER AS THOUGH HE WERE STANDING UPRIGHT WITH HIS LEGS APART."

Ear

Point of shoulder

2nd sacral vertebra

Hip joint

An upright position (standing correctly).

An upright position (riding correctly). (Note the only discernible difference is the bent knee.)

A proud, perpendicular position in the saddle is the hallmark of a great dressage rider. Here, a smiling Dr Reiner Klimke rides his lap of honour on Ahlerich after winning the gold medal at Los Angeles in 1984.

only in dressage, but also for hacking out more safely. Although essentially very different from the jumping position, we see many experienced show jumpers using the classical seat between jumps, collecting their horse prior to facing a particularly awkward obstacle or before negotiating a tricky corner when they may wish suddenly to change legs or to check (half-halt). The Germans are particularly good at this since the majority of German riders have a thorough grounding in classical riding before they branch into the various disciplines. Changing from the jumping position into a deep classical position and back again is relatively simple for the expert, and goes a long way towards explaining why so many top show jumpers ride with a lengthened stirrup leather nowadays. It is axiomatic that it is truly impossible to sit classically with a short stirrup.

Riding in this way was not always so. In the days before the saddle or even the saddle-pad made of animal hides was invented, ancient warriors struggled to ride comfortably on the horse. No doubt we have all experienced as children how razor-sharp a backbone can be on a donkey or pony when we ride bareback. Out of self-protection, the riders of prehistory often rode on the horses' loins, as we see from ancient Assyrian and Egyptian friezes and pottery. But this was damaging for the horse since it is his weakest point, and those cavalrymen had little control of their mounts for the complicated exercises of equestrian combat which were to develop under the Greeks. By the time of Xenophon however, well muscled, "double backed" horses were being selected and a type of saddle had been developed from the shabrack. This made it possible for the cavalryman to ride over the horse's centre of motion, and give him true control with his body. From that time on, man learned how to use his horse to the full, and the wonderful athletic exercises of the manège developed. Thus evolved classical riding.

THE BENEFITS OF A GOOD SEAT

As those ancient Greeks soon discovered, the benefits to the horse of a good seat were all important. Today, it seems we are less enlightened and we would do well to remind ourselves that horses benefit from a good seat by being able to:

1. Use their backs fully and correctly which will in turn
2. Improve their gaits and increase athleticism – which will in turn
3. Make them happier horses, for being comfortable they are able to enjoy their work.

The advantages to the rider of a good seat can be listed as follows:

1. Safety – from greater
2. Control – which leads to
3. Comfort – which brings about
4. Elegance – which inspires
5. Confidence.

There is nothing more beautiful than a correct classical seat which naturally sets the horse off at his best. Horses trained in this way will actually grow in beauty as they develop the correct muscles and transform from mere vehicles into gymnasts. All this is possible for the ordinary horse and rider. There are two more benefits for the rider. On the physical side he will experience:

6. Fitness leading to improved health, and on the mental and spiritual side, a dedicated rider will discover
7. Harmony – that wonderful feeling of being at one with his horse and with Nature.

The riders of prehistory often rode on the horses' loins before the saddle was developed.

Balance, Feel and Rhythm

WHY THEY COUNT BEFORE ALL ELSE

STATE OF MIND

When attempting to go further in riding than mastering the basics of each gait remember that if you are not confident and *happy* in what you are doing, it is unlikely you will be able to exert the degree of control that is required. One of the most difficult ground rules to acquire is the ability to separate and co-ordinate different parts of your body at the same time. Body awareness is not just a cliché dreamed up by the yoga experts. It is an essential state of mind for progressive riding.

With a picture of Xenophon's ideal rider firmly established in our subconscious let us begin now to explore the logic behind the classical seat. There are two governing factors to be considered:

1. BALANCE
2. GRAVITY

The one influences the other.

BALANCE

We should first be clear as to why we give aids to our horses rather than crude signals such as kicking on to break from one gait into a faster one or hauling on the reins to slow down. The difference is that the classical rider applies his aids to complement the natural balance of himself and his horse. The distribution of weight through the rider's trunk, seat and legs specifically directed through correctly applied aids will help the horse to remain in balance *whatever* is asked of him. This will be true whether he is going forwards, sideways or backwards. The secret of such success is a deep, central and upright seat and extremely refined and sensitive aids. If you think how *little* adjustment is made with the steering wheel when driving a high performance, quality motorcar down a busy, winding road this may give an idea of how refined the weight aids should be on horseback.

GRAVITY

Try never to attempt to do on a horse something which goes against gravity. On the contrary, the rider should use gravity to help him sit correctly. Everything which he does happily and easily on the ground should guide him towards knowing what to do on horseback. This should apply to literally every movement. For the inexperienced, the problems normally begin when the rider is required to do something on

Forcing the legs too far back results in the trunk toppling forward.

14

This rider's legs are too far back and her shoulders forward. She has saved herself temporarily with her hands but her imbalance has caused her to lose control of the horse.

horseback which would be difficult for him to carry out even when stationary on the ground. Forcing the legs too far back (or forward) is a good case in point; performed on the ground it would cause imbalance which if not corrected immediately would result in the trunk toppling forward (or backwards).

I know I am not alone in expressing the view that many riders would benefit if first they were given lessons off the horse. Postural behaviour could be noted and much would be gained by the instructor demonstrating certain basic safety requirements which the rider could practise and establish in confidence before making the transition to the saddle.

In our everyday lives, we all use gravity to enable ourselves to carry out certain activities. We do this without thinking. Take the normal standing position. If we allow ourselves to go in front of the vertical and incline our upper bodies forward, we are likely to fall on our noses. Similarly, if we stand with hips sagging, lean backward and round our spines, we may hit the deck with the back of our heads. Self-preservation keeps us remaining perpendicularly upright. We automatically support ourselves, particularly in the back

One of the greatest difficulties in riding is keeping in balance with the movement of the horse.

area, without thinking about it. Why then, we ask, does this not necessarily happen when we mount a horse? The reasons are three-fold:

1. A moving animal is in so many ways an unknown quantity. However outwardly confident the rider, he may suffer inwardly from extreme anxiety about falling off and hurting himself. This is particularly relevant amongst adult riders, especially mothers with young children for whom a bad fall could be catastrophic. These worries therefore cause a general build-up of tension in the muscles which, as we all know, is easily transmitted to the horse.

2. Then there is the added difficulty of keeping in balance with the movement of the horse. Not only does the rider have to balance himself correctly, he must also try to balance himself over the horse's constantly moving centre of gravity.

3. By the very act of taking our feet off the ground to sit astride, we are physically losing some of our most important natural reflexes. Our feet harbour tiny sensors which are activated when we stand on the ground. These sensors give out reflex impulses or messages to the muscles which support the framework of the body.

Thus balance is automatically kept, whatever we are doing on the ground, without any real conscious effort.

BODY AWARENESS

On a horse however, everything changes. Not only our physical reflexes but also our natural inhibitions will bring about a mental block to the process of inbuilt balance. On horseback, balance must be re-learned. This will come very naturally to the confident or the very athletic but there are others who, unwittingly, will feel very much at sea. This is not a question of stubborness or stupidity; it is a very real problem. However, understanding the reason takes us halfway towards putting it right. It is simply a question of making an extra conscious effort. This is where it becomes important to have a clear picture in the mind's eye of what one is trying to achieve. It is easy to say forget about the theory – just feel and it will come right. Feel will only be understood correctly if accompanied by knowledge.

Studying the illustrations which demonstrate an imaginary gravitational plumbline within our bodies is helpful. These complement Xenophon's theory of the classical seat. Begin by practising this posture on the stationary horse. Settle down gently into the saddle and try to imagine the gravity flowing down unimpeded through the checkpoints of your body. Allow your legs to grow long from the hip as the gravity eventually earths itself into the foot. With the upper body try to feel as balanced and upright as you would on the ground. Support your spine! Think proud! This is the first step to body awareness.

The young child does not appear to require the mental application that we have talked about so far. Firstly, he has few inhibitions, for his instincts are still largely primitive. Put a five-year-old who has never ridden before in his life on a horse, and the chances are you will find perfect posture. The body immediately takes up a perpendicular position, the eyes looking forward, the shoulders back, the trunk balanced correctly over the hips, the chest open and the belly relaxed, the upper back will be straight and the lower back slightly curved inwards. The legs will hang down

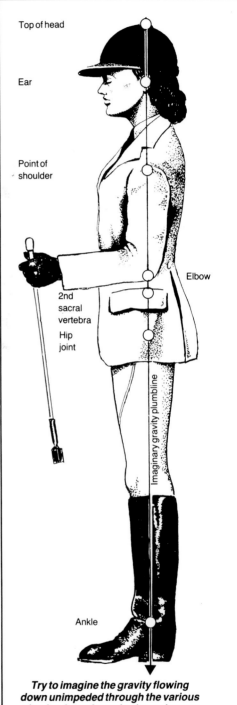

Try to imagine the gravity flowing down unimpeded through the various checkpoints of your body as close as possible to those of the standing figure. Of course much of your weight

Put a five-year-old who has never ridden before on a pony and the chances are you will find a near perfect posture. At this stage the foot is hanging down naturally before the stirrups are placed on the saddle.

Imaginary gravity plumbline

is diverted into the seat bones when you ride, but the gravity displacement should not be very great. A constant picture of the imaginary plumbline is therefore very helpful.

loose and long with minimal tension.

It is important at this stage when the horse is led forward that the child continues to support himself in the back. If he relaxes too much he may wobble and lose balance. There must be as much self-carriage in his postition on the horse, stationary or moving, as there would be if he were standing upright or actively running about. The neck, back and chest must at all times support themselves.

One of the novice trainer's biggest mistakes is to command a class of pupils . . . "Everyone relax!" Taken literally, this could not be worse – especially during the trot or worse still the canter. The upper body would not remain upright if really relaxed, and riders would benefit much better from simply being told to sit up straight. It is important however to think in terms of dividing the body into two parts. The upper part, i.e. from the waist upwards, must be constantly supportive of itself. The lower part, ie. from the waist downwards, should be more relaxed and mould itself to the horse. *Mentally tell yourself your lower body has become part of the horse.*

With that thought uppermost the trainer should check that his pupils are in fact sitting squarely. Not on the fork, not on the back of the buttocks, but on the whole seat. Provided that the back is well supported and the checkpoints as illustrated are maintained, this should happen fairly naturally. Now the pupil is in a position to ride on from the seat. If the novice rider merely concentrates on where he wishes to go, he will probably achieve this from his normal body reactions. "Ride with your body!" is easily understood by beginners and is more important than giving detailed explanations of seat, hand and leg aids at this stage. We shall deal with the mechanics of the back and the pelvis in the next chapter, but there are two useful observations to be made beforehand in our general study of the overall position.

Firstly, that the more 'civilised' or urbanised the rider, the more difficult it appears for him to achieve a good natural posture at the beginning. He has

This Portuguese campino has probably never had a riding lesson, yet he sits proud and erect and has perfect control over his horse.

got to work hard at achieving it which, in some cases, may take years of reading, receiving instruction and practical experience on many different types of horse. With patience and above all open-mindedness however, good posture and a sense of balance will develop in time. For a few, the process may be rapid – there are always naturals in every sport – particularly if they are fortunate enough to learn on a really good schoolmaster horse. For others, it may take years to feel truly at one with the horse. As so many of the great Masters of equitation have pointed out through the ages, you have to work and work and work at achieving a good seat. This is as much mental as physical, and sadly there is no magic formula. But the path may be made smoother and clearer if the correct guidelines are laid down from the beginning.

It perhaps seems unfair that the man who lives a more primitive lifestyle than today's average sporting rider, appears to adopt a fair version of the classical seat without ever having had a day's lesson. For him indeed this is acquired by instinct and feel alone. American Indians, Mexican cowboys, Portuguese and Spanish stockmen all possess a beautiful natural seat. What is more, their bearing is as

proud as a highly trained rider at the Spanish Riding School. Why? The answer can be discovered by watching the women of rural India or the Australians or African bush to realise that somewhere, somehow along the line, we in the West have lost the God-given, proud self-carriage. Therefore, over civilised, bowed down as we are by too much sedentary work or worries about the mortgage, we usually have to learn to use our bodies again. Self-inflicted tension is the enemy of natural posture both on the ground and on horseback.

My second observation amongst our modern society is that those people who dance well and have a natural sense of rhythm normally make excellent dressage pupils. Not only do they feel for the rhythm of the horse in all his gaits, they are also able to co-ordinate their bodies to the extent that they can quite happily 'separate' their pelvis from their trunk.

Riding is all about rhythm. The body must be trained to 'listen' to the rhythm of the horse. In the beginning, this is best done on the lunge on a blanket with the eyes shut. With the horse in walk, the rider will gradually recognise the feeling under his seat as each step is taken. The sensation under his buttocks as the horse's back rises when each hindfoot touches the ground and pushes up to come forward again will start to register. In this way the rudiments of an understanding for the rhythm of the horse will be established. Ideally, the rider should not progress beyond the all-important, preliminary lunge-work until he can recognise which hoof (or hooves) is striking the ground in all three gaits. This takes time but it is well worth while and only then will he be truly acquainted with *feel*.

The Back and the Pelvis

A DEEPER AWARENESS

The best advice I ever had was from an elderly pianist who had spent most of his life playing music for people to dance to, from traditional ballet to the most up-to-date disco-dance. He always said the same thing: "Shoulders back and still! Back straight but supported! Then move from the hips with the beat!" This is as applicable to the rider as it is to the dancer With regard to really athletic disco-dance, black people undoubtedly make the best dancers; then come the Latins, and trailing a long way behind in rhythmic dancing come the more phlegmatic races of the North. But those latter who have mastered the inhibitions of the naturally cautious often emerge with a brilliance all of their own simply because they have worked at it.

You may not like soul music but gyrating to a Top Ten record with a good basic beat in front of a long mirror does wonders for understanding the potential of the body in relation to sitting on a horse. The secret – as my old friend said – is to keep the shoulders absolutely still and back, and allow the hips to move in any direction you care to make.

At this stage, thinking riders may ask two very relevant questions.

1. Why should we try to keep the trunk upright and still?
2. Why is it so vital to move from the hips?

The answer to the first may seem commonsense to some but over amplification of this basic principle will only add to our understanding of the second question.

We have already talked about balance in a previous chapter, but it is not always

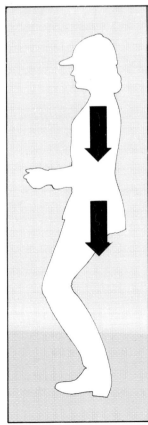

appreciated that an erect upper body will increase the downward, central pressure and thereby the stability of the seat. Commandant Jean Licart, former écuyer to the famous Cadre Noir at Saumur in France, sums up the position of the upper body quite simply in his book, *Basic Equitation** . . . "To be a good rider, you must stay on the horse *through the erectness and balance of the trunk.*" Anyone who has given a child or friend a pick-a-back will appreciate the importance of stillness in the trunk. If the burden

---

* *Basic Equitation* by Commandant Jean Licart, J.A. Allen and Co. Ltd., London, 1976 edition.

The erectness of the upper body increases the downward central pressure on the seat and thereby improves the rider's stability in the saddle.

wavers and moves its shoulders about, it is almost impossible to achieve any degree of equilibrium. It is exactly the same for the horse. The upper body of the rider is his balancing pole, and for the horse to remain in balance, only very minute movements will be tolerated. A sudden shift forward (or back) – often caused by the rider suddenly lowering his head – may upset his balance. Once the horse drops onto the forehand all true rider influence will be lost.

FLEXIBILITY

Recently a well-known dressage rider and writer suggested to me that too much flexibility in the rider's hip could damage the horse's back. This brings me to answering the second question which is absolutely fundamental to our understanding of a good seat and the ideals of classical riding, i.e. to be in harmony with a horse. Moreover, this vital point is often overlooked as it would seem from the short conversation reported

This rider is able to sit still and centrally into her saddle despite the bouncy nature of the trot. This is becase she is mobile in the hip joint and the spine retains its natural curve in the lower back, allowing the muscles round the loins to absorb the movement of the horse (see text).

above.

In our attempts to establish a good riding position, we must never lose sight of the fact that a horse is a living, moving thing. As Licart very neatly points out therefore, "The seat is inseparable from the idea of movement."

One does not need to be a rider to know that a rigid body on top of a moving, bouncing, staccato body will be jolted, banged and jarred unless at some point or junction there is a mechanism which can give. In the wonderfully engineered human frame, riders are blessed with the hip joint and the elasticity of the lower back or loins which allows the pelvis to move gently and sensitively with the horse. Suppleness in this area is therefore of paramount importance and should at all times be encouraged – never stifled. This flexibility allows the rider not so much to 'follow' the action of his horse, but to become part of it. Once he has learned to tune into the horse's own rhythm, he may then invite the horse in any direction he wishes through subtle weight aids. By so doing the classical rider and his horse move as one.

When a horse moves forward, the action of his hindlegs stepping underneath his body, the swinging of his back, and the elevation and stretching forward of his forelimbs all combine to throw the rider about. If the rider is locked in the hip, he will be unable to absorb the movement of the horse through the muscles in the small of his back and therefore his whole frame will be momentarily dislodged from the saddle. This will lead to an uncomfortable bumping of the entire trunk. Down as the hindlegs come forward to step underneath; up as they touch the ground. The result – which can still be seen far too often all over the country at every level of riding? A harsh bang, bang, bang with the rider's seat on the horse's back.

Consider, by contrast, the rider who is mobile in the hip joint, who is supple in the lower back, and who has learned to move the pelvis independently of the trunk, i.e. the rider who can keep the shoulders back and still, the upper back straight, and who, like the disco-dancer, can separate and move the hips or pelvis.

This rider, by virtue of his suppleness, is in a position to remain at one with his horse. The very freedom of his pelvis from the locked position to the supple mobility required by the dancer, enables him to sit quietly on his horse and appear to the onlooker to be absolutely still in the saddle. Like the dancer he is in rhythm and this is the paradox of good riding. Stillness and quietness in the saddle may only be achieved by suppleness and the ability to move and, more important, be moved

in the pelvic area.

Unfortunately, however, countless people are locked into one permanent position which makes it very difficult for them to use their bodies to maximum potential. There are few people who can kick their own height or even near it, and even less who can do the splits. There is no need perhaps to go to these extremes in order to achieve mobility of the hip but most people would be greatly helped by taking some form of exercise on the ground to ensure suppleness in the hip joint before progressing to higher aims in their riding. So much human backpain would be alleviated if more attention was paid to the subject of pelvic flexibility, and contrary to what my learned friend was suggesting, so many horses' backs would be spared.

The Greeks certainly had the right idea when they laid down the rules for good riding. By simulating the standing position in the saddle i.e. with pelvis upright or almost upright, with the upper back straight and flat, with the shoulders back and down, and the spine retaining its natural curve in the lower back, an independent seat should not be difficult to achieve.

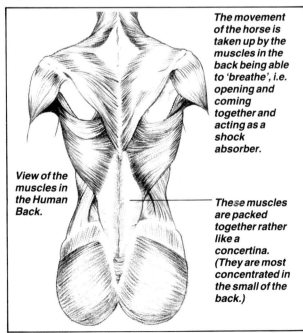

The movement of the horse is taken up by the muscles in the back being able to 'breathe', i.e. opening and coming together and acting as a shock absorber.

View of the muscles in the Human Back.

These muscles are packed together rather like a concertina. (They are most concentrated in the small of the back.)

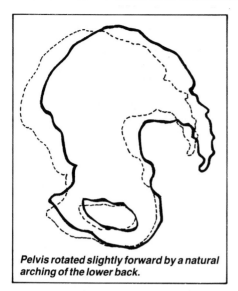

Pelvis rotated slightly forward by a natural arching of the lower back.

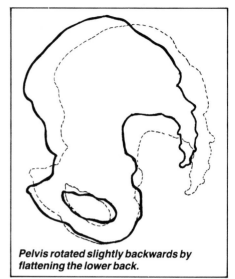

Pelvis rotated slightly backwards by flattening the lower back.

MUSCULAR CONTROL

The muscles in the small of the back are not large but they are extremely effective. It is comparatively easy to 'lengthen' (stretch) or to 'shorten' (contract) these muscles in order to influence the pelvis a few inches forward or back. What is difficult is allowing this to happen. Bodies which have grown lazy in everyday performance on the ground, will also be lazy on horseback. As mentioned before, one often has to work at attaining a good seat, yet the work itself is not strenuous. It is much more a case of application.

Subtlety is the name of the game in riding, and the pelvis must be as quiet in its flexibility as all the other aids. A rough, over-active seat will do as much or more damage as rough hands. Softness and tact must be present at all times.

As already suggested, dancing to a good soul beat is also excellent provided that you remember to keep an erect upper back with the eyes looking forward. As you gyrate, keeping the upper back as still as possible, experiment a little. You will find that you can rotate the pelvis clockwise, anti-clockwise, forwards, backwards and sideways and it is important to discover which muscles in the small of the back achieve which effect. Place your fingers

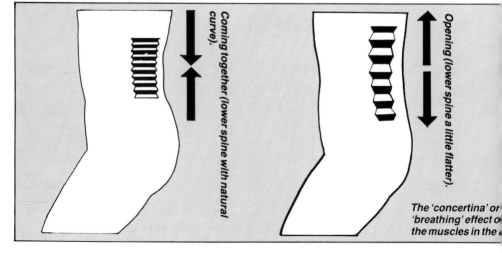

Coming together (lower spine with natural curve).

Opening (lower spine a little flatter).

The 'concertina' or 'breathing' effect o the muscles in the

lightly on these muscles so that you are able to connect the feeling in the lower back with the result you achieve in the pelvis.

Not only do these small muscles aid flexibility in the pelvis, they also act as shock absorbers against sudden jarring or stress. One of the most difficult gaits to sit to in the saddle is the medium trot. The horse whose hocks are well engaged will throw a stiff rider about in no uncertain fashion and the result is uncomfortable in the extreme for both partners. The tendency is to start to grip and the elasticity of the back is lost. If however the rider is able to sit in balance with his seat bones well underneath him and his upper body in correct alignment over his hips, the pliancy of the spine in the loin area will allow him to remain as though glued to the saddle. This is brought about by a shock absorber effect in the muscles just above the pelvis and also in the buttocks themselves provided that they are evenly spread over the saddle.

These back muscles can best be described as being packed together rather like a concertina. They will allow the required movement in the pelvic area by their 'breathing' action as they lengthen and contract, taking up the full movement of the gait. They can only do this provided that the pelvis remains in as *upright* a position as possible and that the rider is mentally relaxed enough not to tense up round the stomach and suck it inwards. It is not generally known by the layman that the

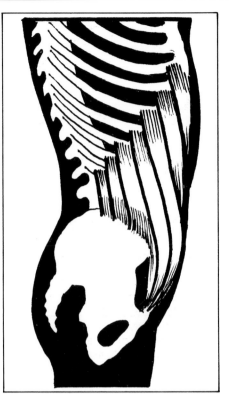

The attachment of the abdominal muscles to the pelvis (see text).

long abdominal muscles (see above) stretch downwards to attach themselves at their extremity to the pubic bone. Therefore when the tummy muscles tighten they tilt the pubis upwards and the top of the pelvis backwards thereby flattening the small of the back. When over-relaxed they destroy the support of the lower back. The idea is to soften forward but maintain support, thus allowing the pelvis to remain in its natural upright position.

THE BACK

Feel will help the rider to develop this very refined control of the pelvis through the small of the back and the abdominal muscles. Writers refer to the accentuated use of the muscles in the loin area as 'bracing the back', but this can be misleading as different writers interpret this expression in different ways. The English and Germans normally imply a stretching of the loin muscles when they speak of 'bracing'; whilst the Austrian, Spanish,

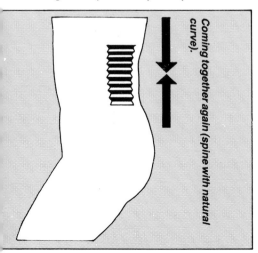

Coming together again (spine with natural curve).

(Photo by courtesy of Madeleine McCurley.)

Portuguese and French Schools tend to expand the chest and stomach area by accentuating the curve of the lower back, i.e. by tightening the loin muscles. A general view of this important situation is probably best summed up by a section in the FEI dressage rules (Article 417 para 2, 1983) which states: "Only the rider who understands how to contract and relax his loin muscles at the right moment is able to influence his horse correctly."

To understand how to use our backs more efficiently, let us consider again Xenophon's standing/riding position. The importance here is the angle of the pelvis. In the correct standing position when viewed from the side, the pelvis is roughly upright – neither tilted back or forward. In fact at around *0 degree tilt. From now on in this book we shall refer to this as our Basic Position.

It is important to have a neutral starting point for all our riding. Therefore the description Basic Position is self-explanatory. It gives us the feeling for a

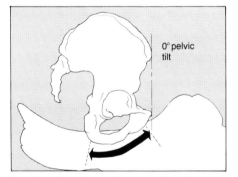

The French and Latin interpretation of 'bracing the back' shows an upright posture of the pelvis which distributes the weight more evenly over the whole seat. Note this rider on his Lusitano stallion is sitting well forward which allows the horse to soften in the back and lower the quarters for the more collected movements.

position to which we will always return before making certain adjustments for specific movements. It could be likened to the neutral gear position in a car. It is also

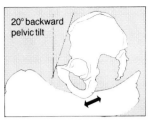

The German or Scandinavian method of 'bracing the back' shows the pelvis tilted well back behind the vertical. This position engages the seatbones more deeply and is effective for driving the horse forward. It could, however, aggravate a less robust horse's back.

the 'allowing' position for a gait which has been attained and requires no further adjustment save for a quiet encouragement forward with the legs.

In the Basic Position the rider will be carried lightly and interfere less with the horse's movement than in any other position provided always that the rest of the body is correctly carried in alignment. From this position it is easiest of all for the spine to flex. In free, forward gaits, the pelvis will rotate slightly clockwise. In the more collected gaits, the rider may wish to ease the weight from the seatbones towards the fork by rotating the pelvis slightly forward.

The Germans have a word – 'Kreuz' – which literally means small of the back. With 'Kreuz', we read how they are able to transform horses which are heavy on the forehand and drag their hindquarters into veritable gymnasts, light in the hand and deeply engaged behind. There is no real magic to 'Kreuz'. It is simply a matter of developing the muscles in the lower back and by feel knowing when and how to use them and what effect the rotational influence of the pelvis will have on the horse. Obviously, no back aid will work without the required interplay of hand and leg which is only gained with time and patience.

This excerpt from an article written by Anthony Crossley for *Riding* Magazine on the subject of the back followed a visit he made some years ago to the cradle of classical riding, the Iberian Peninsula. That great classical riding maestro of modern

times, the Portuguese Mestre Nuno Oliveira clearly impressed him. "The theory of the use of the back is a subject that has been all too frequently misunderstood or totally neglected in this country and therein may lie the greatest single cause of our current weakness as dressage riders. It must suffice here to say that whereas most British riders, operating as they do without effective back influence, are rather too well known for their inability to collect their horses, Nuno Oliveira, riding primarily with an unusually strong and well-controlled back, is famous as a regular producer of some of the best collected and lightest horses in the world."

Since, as Colonel Crossley rightly points out, the use of the back is all too easily neglected perhaps this chapter will go some way towards redressing the balance. The main point of which we must not lose sight is to allow the lower back to retain its natural curve for the majority of work. Some instructors will place a riding stick between the rider's elbows whilst he is taken on the lunge to maintain the curve inwards from the loins; others ask the rider for an 'arch' by stretching and expanding the chest and lowering and advancing the belly. There are no hard and fast rules, but by far the best way to learn the influences of the back and pelvis is to sit on an advanced schoolmaster horse whose response to the aids will give the pupil a feel he will always remember.

*This position was so named and discussed in detail in an excellent article which first appeared in *Horse and Rider* in November 1986, by John Gorman.

The Seat
WHAT DOES IT REALLY INVOLVE?

OUR HERITAGE

Today's interpretation of the classical seat owes much if not all to the French School of the 18th Century. Approximately, two thousand years after Xenophon wrote his famous treatise on equitation, the French royal écuyer, Sieur François Robichon de la Guerinière came to the forefront of classical riding in Europe. He introduced the new flat *selle à la francaise* which was to reform past theories and allow a bent 'breathing' leg instead of a straight stretched one. In the recently published *Advanced Techniques of Riding* produced by the German National Equestrian Federation as their official riding handbook, we read how: "This saddle enabled the development of the modern seat, based on both seat bones and the crotch." Thus La Guerinière left us with a logical study of the art of schooling which has given us the guidelines for dressage today.

On the Continent, where *haute école* is kept alive and pursued by many thousands of people, Guerinière's style is still vigorously emanated. In England however, as cross-country riding developed and little emphasis was placed upon manège riding, the classical seat of the School of Versailles

was virtually lost. Saddles altered drastically to complement the new up and forward seat of the hunting field. In the two hundred odd years of its existence, this seat eclipsed all that had gone before and Classical Riding became a forgotten art.

Little wonder therefore that teaching the use of the seat as an aid has become a controversial subject! In the Forward Seat, the weight of the rider was predominantly on the stirrups as he leant towards the withers; the seat was rarely in contact except at walk. Rising or 'posting' to the trot was the norm and for many it is still unthinkable or impossible to sit comfortably to the trot or canter.

Despite the recent growth of the dressage industry, instructors in England are still retiscent to teach the use of the seat no doubt influenced by our past. It is often left to instructors who have trained abroad to help those who wish to go further in their riding. A good seat is the basis of all school riding in countries such as Austria, Germany, France, Portugal and Spain and it is considered the first and foremost aid.

La Guerinière (1688-1751) was probably the first person of importance to adopt the all-embracing seat with the bent, 'breathing' leg which he taught to all his pupils.

A FEEL FOR WHAT IS RIGHT

The 'born rider' will not require detailed explanations. The use of the seat will come naturally to him through feel. There are others however who benefit from discussion and dialogue particularly concerning the simple functioning of the body. It is comforting to know that using the seat efficiently and correctly directs strain away from the vulnerable human spine and a good rider should never have back problems – at least not from riding.

If we would all act naturally on horseback, the following five chapters would become superfluous. We have already suggested that: **When you ride, you should in principle do on the horse what you would do on the ground.**

If you doubt the wisdom of this, try answering the following simple tests with reference to everyday life on the ground.

1. In what position is your pelvis when you walk forward?

2. What happens to your weight when you go sideways?

3. In what position is your pelvis when you walk backwards?

4. If you canter (skip) which leg comes back to push you forward onto a right lead?

5. And which hip bone is slightly in advance when you get going?

6. If you walk a small circle, in which direction is your weight directed?

7. If you are walking smartly forwards and you wish to pull up suddenly, what do you do with your back and pelvis?

8. For jogging efficiently on the spot or on flat ground, would your pelvis be upright, tilted forward or backwards?

If you work it out, you will find the answers to all these questions are in each case akin to the involuntary movements you make in the saddle.

Answers:
1. Upright or just a little behind the vertical;
2. In the direction in which you wish to go;
3. Tipped slightly forward (crotch down);
4. The left;
5. The right;

6. To the inside;
7. Your lower back arches a little forward which rotates your pelvis a little forward and down;
8. Upright.

These are all normal body movements, and the main activity takes place in the pelvic area the moment the request is transmitted from the brain. Try it and see for yourself. Nobody taught you how to do these things on the ground. Your responses are governed by instinct through balance.

If you can transfer all these responses to the horse, then there is little need for you to continue with this book. It should all, after all, be a matter of feel, i.e. the movement you make in the pelvis will manifest itself on the saddle through your seat.

For those, however, who desire a clear definition of the seat, let us therefore go back to basics and discuss the true meaning. In general terms, we talk about a good riding seat to summarise the overall picture of the rider. This includes head, neck, shoulders, back, arms, legs and finally his true seat, or bottom. To define the latter, let us from now on call this part of our anatomy the Seat with a capital S.

The Seat forms the broad base of support under our bodies when we sit down in the saddle. We may sit in a variety of ways, but for work on the flat we are concerned with the safest and most efficient position for influencing the horse underneath us. It is vital that this position will allow us the greatest freedom of our legs for use as effective and discerning aids; it should also enable us to sit as quietly as possible in order for the horse to remain in balance.

By emulating Xenophon and La Guerinière's idea of the upright figure in the saddle, i.e. the Basic Position, it is virtually impossible not to become aware of a triangular area of support under the body. When we stretch our legs well open and bring them back into a semi-perpendicular position, this has the effect of allowing the pelvis to settle deeply into place unimpeded by fat or muscle. There will be a slight tilting backwards when we take up our stirrups, but provided that these are not excessively short and the lower leg is kept back, it is possible to maintain the upright pelvis simply by supporting the spine upwards, opening the chest and advancing the waist. **Depth and openess of seat are all important here.**

THE CHAIR SEAT

Before pursuing this deeply balanced Seat, let us consider the other options open to us. Through no fault of their own, many people – particularly if accustomed to a forward cut jumping saddle, never really stretch their legs open and back. These are the back of the thigh sitters, and I am ashamed to say that for at least the first ten years of my riding life, I fell into this category. It is perfectly possible to sit down on the fleshy muscular part at the rear of the thighs and balance on the back of the two seat bones. With a shortened stirrup and the lower leg thrust somewhat forward, a fairly secure position is achieved by virtue of the pressure against the stirrup. This Seat may be quite adequate for going fast across country provided that a) the horse underneath is active and forward going and b) there is little danger of a bad buck, or peck or fall at a jump. It is not however adequate to control or satisfactorily push on an evasive or recalcitrant horse without resorting to excessive use of leg, spur or crop. From

Not only is the back of the buttocks seat inefficient; it may also be damaging to the horse's back as it presses down on the loins. Yet, all too many experienced riders still adopt this seat.

the safety angle, one must have a highly developed sense of balance to save oneself in an emergency. Many chair sitters will be in severe trouble if at speed they lose a stirrup, or, far worse, if a leather breaks. Then all true security will be lost.

It is time now to concentrate on the most efficient posture in the saddle, our Basic Position from which we may learn to ride classically. For maximum control, an all-embracing seat which is independent of the stirrups is by far the safest. It should be noted here however that a suitable saddle is a must. Whilst the majority of the continental riders have never diverged from the use of an all-purpose saddle for *campagne* and school riding, many of us at home have been brought up to believe that the old-fashioned hunting saddle or more modern models based on a similar

28

This exemplary picture from the Spanish Riding School of Colonel Podhajsky clearly shows the all-embracing nature of the upright seat with a frontal contact of the fork and thighs visibly shown. (Photo reproduced by kind permission of Eva Podhajsky from The Complete Training of Horse & Rider written by Colonel Podhajsky.)

Despite the fact that this rider is leaning forward, there is no snug contact with the saddle from the fork and thighs. Indeed, the calves are gripping up and the rider's weight is on the rear of the thighs.

construction (including even early versions of the Pony Club saddle) automatically place one in the correct position. This is wishful thinking.

In his definitive book, *The Country Life Book of Saddlery,* Elwyn Hartley-Edwards describes the hunting seat "leg thrust forward and seat to the rear of the saddle" as "notorious". This was caused, he goes on to write, as a "result of badly designed saddles rather than of any conscious effort by the rider."

THE RIGHT WAY

Fortunately for the horse, all the great masters of equitation are unanimous in the cultivation of a central Seat which brings the rider into balance with the horse's own centre of balance.

Assuming therefore that:

1. We sit in a saddle which comfortably allows this central balance—and

2. We have, through exercises (on the ground and the lunge) become supple in the hipjoint, we should by now be in a position to appreciate what is meant by the Three Point Seat.

The expression 'three point seat' is one of imagery. It indicates a broad base of support represented by the entire pelvic floor rather than being isolated to the back of the seatbones only, sometimes known as a 'two point seat'. Look at the diagram which shows the rough triangle of the pelvic floor. This is biological fact although bad saddle design prevents many riders from discovering it. Only from a broad, flattish saddle twist will the rider relax and 'open' the seat to appreciate the two long ischial ridges which extend forward under the perineum (supporting all the vital organs) and which fuse in front to form the inferior pubic arch—the

third point. Contact throughout this entire area leads to far greater support for the pelvis, the abdomen and ultimately the rider's spine which in the two point position is more vulnerable to jarring.

Classical riders, ancient and modern, have defined this all-round contact in similar vein. William Frazer's 1801 translation from La Guerinière states: "Let the horseman then place himself upon his twist [fork] sitting exactly in the middle of the saddle; let him support this posture in which the twist alone seems to sustain the weight of the whole body by moderately leaning upon his buttocks, let his thighs be turned inwards and rest *flat* upon the sides of his saddle, and in order to do this, let the turn of the thighs proceed directly from the hips."

Bobinsky, a Russian colonel, wrote in 1836: "Lean back with the upper part of the torso and push the belt and stomach forward; sit resting on . . . the two seat bones and the crotch. These points . . . form the base of the rider's position . . ."

Charles Harris, an Englishman, formerly with the Spanish Riding School in Austria, wrote for *Light Horse* in 1953 .that the rider should sit on ". . . a triangular base" composed of the two buttocks and "the crutch which acts merely as a steadier and not a 'perch'".

A. K. Frederiksen, the Danish cavalry instructor wrote in 1969, "The rider must sit rather forward in the deepest part of the saddle. His weight must be on the two pelvic bones . . . and the crotch, that is three points of support."

Finally the latest German Official Handbook states "The foundation of the seat has three points: the two seat bones and the crotch."

There is therefore nothing new or revolutionary about the three point seat, but it is noteworthy that the older the rider becomes, the

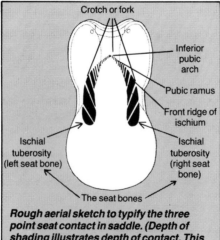

Rough aerial sketch to typify the three point seat contact in saddle. (Depth of shading illustrates depth of contact. This can of course be varied according to what the rider requests from the horse.)

Crotch or fork

Inferior pubic arch

Pubic ramus

Front ridge of ischium

Ischial tuberosity (left seat bone)

Ischial tuberosity (right seat bone)

The seat bones

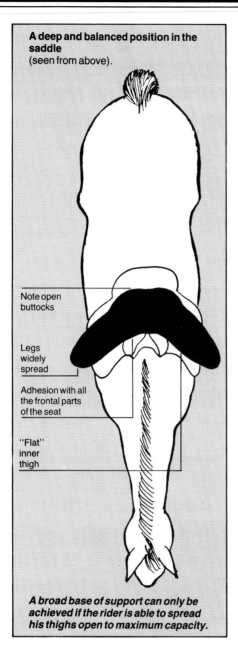

A deep and balanced position in the saddle
(seen from above).

Note open buttocks

Legs widely spread

Adhesion with all the frontal parts of the seat

"Flat" inner thigh

A broad base of support can only be achieved if the rider is able to spread his thighs open to maximum capacity.

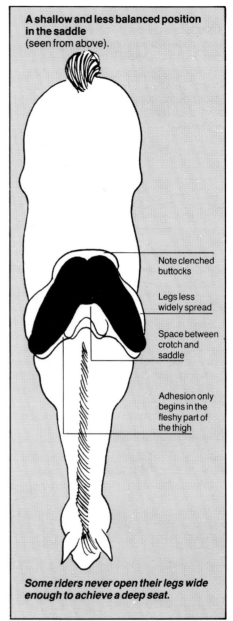

A shallow and less balanced position in the saddle
(seen from above).

Note clenched buttocks

Legs less widely spread

Space between crotch and saddle

Adhesion only begins in the fleshy part of the thigh

Some riders never open their legs wide enough to achieve a deep seat.

more difficult it is to attain, due to stiffness in the hipjoint. Sadly, this difficulty has caused some of our more venerable equestrians to change their views and attack this well documented principle.

Apart from stability and comfort for the horse, the three point seat allows the subtle use of weight aids. As the pelvis is joined to the spine in such a way that the seatbones are lower than the crotch, the rider's weight will be naturally exerted towards those points, which help to encourage or 'push' the horse onward as they work forward under the rider's body in harmony with the horse's own forward movement.

The pelvis viewed from the front.

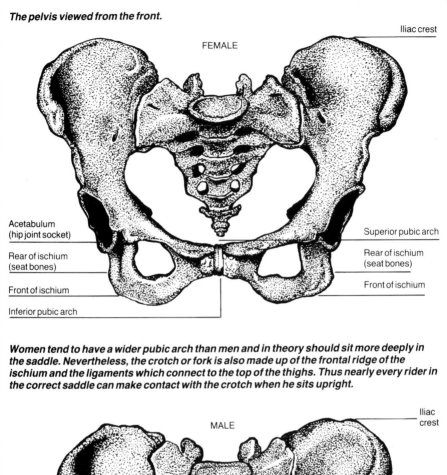

FEMALE

Iliac crest

Acetabulum
(hip joint socket)

Rear of ischium
(seat bones)

Front of ischium

Inferior pubic arch

Superior pubic arch

Rear of ischium
(seat bones)

Front of ischium

Women tend to have a wider pubic arch than men and in theory should sit more deeply in the saddle. Nevertheless, the crotch or fork is also made up of the frontal ridge of the ischium and the ligaments which connect to the top of the thighs. Thus nearly every rider in the correct saddle can make contact with the crotch when he sits upright.

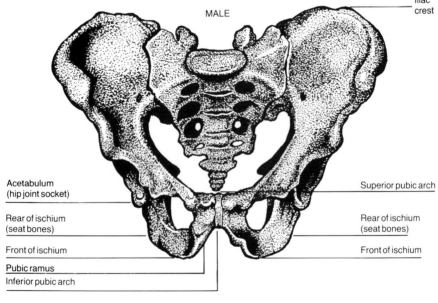

MALE

Iliac
crest

Acetabulum
(hip joint socket)

Rear of ischium
(seat bones)

Front of ischium

Pubic ramus

Inferior pubic arch

Superior pubic arch

Rear of ischium
(seat bones)

Front of ischium

It is the contact with the crotch or fork which gives the rider extra control and security and is vitally important for the more advanced work on the flat. Pressure here acts rather like a handbrake if used too strongly. Discerningly used it acts, in the words of Mr. Harris, as a "steadier". It is important however to avoid saddles which have a high, narrow twist and the best saddles are those which are relatively flat in the twist. Contrary to popular belief the vital organs emerge just above the pubic arch.

Due, however, to the fact that there is a marked difference in the degree of pelvic tilt in relation to the angle of the spine where it joins the pelvis amongst different people, the experts are not always in agreement as to the degree of contact attained here.

Too much analysis of anatomical differences will serve little. **What is far more important is that the rider is aware of sitting on the largest possible area of contacting surfaces which will bring about a greater degree of adhesion in the saddle.** Therefore whether you think of the Seat as roughly triangular in shape, whether you prefer to think of it as three pointed, or whether you consider it to be an undefined area of bony base is perhaps irrelevant. Of far more significance is that the rider should sit well-forward and deep with as little flesh as possible between him and the horse. In this way the rider will grow to recognise the restraining influences of the Seat as well as the forward-driving influences.

Using the lower back muscles to influence the Seat can bring about two effects.

1. It may either encourage the horse forward by indirectly massaging and helping the muscles in the horse's back to soften and stretch, thus increasing activity in the legs;
2. It may stem, steady, direct or even arrest the impulsion of the horse coupled with a restraining hand.

Colonel Handler of Vienna wrote, the Seat is used to drive the horse forward, or ". . . to restrain him. Since each of the aids offers considerable diversity in intensity, point of contact, and direction of stimulus, a whole scale of possible combinations may be used by the rider to affect given muscles and achieve the desired movement of his mount."

It cannot therefore be stressed more strongly how all of these aids should be subtle and quiet. It may take years of learning before one can adequately understand the aids of the back, Seat and weight and it is vital to learn from a good instructor on a schoolmaster horse – always starting off on the lunge to develop the necessary awareness of feel.

Once you have mastered the tremendous feeling of control generated from the deep balanced Seat, tension and worry fall away. Riding becomes so much more effortless and comfortable! Consider the following quotation from *Riding Logic* by Wilhelm Müseler concerning the rider who has learned true control from the Seat by activating his back muscles. It is clear from the text that comfort for the horse and safety for the rider is of paramount importance in the cultivation of the Classical Seat.

"This results in a very close contact with the horse and at the same time, enables the rider to avoid bumping in the saddle and being left behind. He remains firmly seated on the three points; he can at any time influence his horse, stop, turn or urge him on. He will also remain in the saddle if the horse pecks and in the case of a sudden stop or startle can push the horse forward; in short – he can control his horse."

So many people imagine that such a Seat is beyond them; but this is so untrue. Telling a rider to open his chest, bring his shoulders back a little, and really *straighten up* will often bring about the required back action which he will immediately feel in his pelvis. I have often seen the look of amazement in a rider's face when by this simple act he feels the whole of the Seat coming into contact with the horse, rather than just perching on the back of the seat bones. In less time than it takes to tell, this discovery will transform that person into a rider instead of a passenger. Only at this point, will the rider discover the driving forward impulse of his Seat, and those precious restraining influences discussed by Handler of Austria, Müseler of Germany, Henriquet of France, Oliveira of Portugal and countless other classical riders of today. Used with sensitivity and tact, true awareness of the Seat aids will lead to inspired confidence.

The Seat
PUTTING IT ALL INTO PRACTICE

"Riding is the simplest thing in the world and the hardest thing to do well" is an expression we sometimes hear from the top trainers.

It is the simplicity of riding that is so often forgotten. Now that we have discussed at some length the history, the importance and the definition of the Classical Seat, let us progress to discovering its sensation and uses for ourselves.

The Seat is our most natural aid. It constitutes a close, secret language between the horse and ourselves.

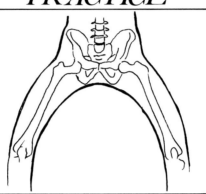

There is a horizontal section at the top of the femur or thigh bone which permits the rider to open his legs wide and settle into a deep, all-embracing seat provided that the legs hang downwards from the hip within the perpendicular framework.

difference between the saddle and chair is that the saddle is *shaped* and you have to straddle it. It should be deep in the centre to accommodate the seat bones; it should rise up in front towards the pommel to accommodate the crotch. A good saddle is designed not only to fit the shape of the horse's back but also that of the human pelvis.

Bearing in mind all that we have learned so far about balance and feel and with a picture of that

In order of importance the aids are comprised of the Seat, the Legs and the Hands. Let us study again the diagrams on pages 30 and 31 which illustrate the Basic Position in the saddle. Unless he is aware of that entire, adhesive spread of the Seat, the rider will never truly be able to influence his horse without a very much stronger hand and leg than is desirable.

important gravitational plumbline in our heads, there are a number of simple exercises, mental and physical, that can be employed to help us sit deeply in the saddle and discover the fullest possible contact of the whole Seat.

1. Before sitting down, stand up in your stirrups and be aware that your legs are as wide apart at the top as possible. If you have plump thighs, use your hand to pull away the fleshy part as you sit down – then tuck it out of the way behind your thigh bone. This will enable your thigh to lie *flatly* against the saddle flap once seated and a snug contact will be made with the whole fork.

ATTAINING DEPTH OF SEAT WHEN THE HORSE IS STATIONARY

To ensure depth of Seat in practice, first *pause* a moment when you get on your horse. Now think about a deep, close, all-embracing Seat. However obvious it may sound, remind yourself that you are not sitting on a chair. The important

It may sound odd, but most people who ride never open their thighs sufficiently wide! This is why they never attain a broad base of support under their bodies. Instead, they have to rely on permanently gripping calves and thighs which are detrimental to sensitive, balanced riding. When the upper leg grips, the muscles will bunch up under the thigh bone, pushing the frame of the rider actually away from the saddle. Therefore the thigh must lie close but relaxed against the saddle. This allows the gravitational force to flow downwards through the body, unrestricted by tense, tightened muscles.

2. Remember that, mechanically, the legs are able to operate best and at their full capacity when the pelvis is upright or almost upright. Check therefore that you are sitting in the Basic Position with the pelvis tipped neither forward nor back. Soften and advance the stomach and grow upwards from the waist! This will help the horse to remain still.

3. Now check that you are indeed sitting evenly and firmly on the Seat bones. (If in doubt as to their whereabouts, slip a hand under each buttock and feel that hard bony roundness of the ball and socket joint where the top of the leg joins the pelvis.) They should be well down and forward in the saddle

bearing the main pressure of the trunk.

Never lose sight of the fact that it is very easy to become a one-sided rider, which will ultimately damage the horse's back. You can normally see the result of one-sided pressure in the sweat marks on a horse's back when you take off the saddle. This is caused by the rider collapsing a hip and not being evenly supported by the muscles in his lower back.

4. Open your buttocks! Remember that once the horse is in motion, you will feel a separate movement in each seat bone as each hindleg strikes the ground and then pushes upward for the next stride forward. To help your body absorb this movement, the buttocks must be open and wide and

A common fault. The rider has rounded her back and is sitting on her 'tail'. This has weakened her position so she has compensated by tensing the shoulder and forearm, and the hands are set.

relaxed.

The exercises emphasised above should help to bring about a positive understanding of what the great Masters refer to as the Classical Seat. Once this is physically felt, understood, and has given the rider an extra feeling of security, there are some additional thoughts to consider.

Instructors should never lose sight of the fact that everyone is built differently. What is possible for Mr. or Ms. Average may be very difficult for others. Skinny people with narrow hips will find that there is little

covering to protect and cushion the base of the pelvis-from wherever it is placed. This is another sound reason for choosing to ride whenever possible in a comfortable saddle. Those people should not be tempted to roll off the seat bones and onto the 'tail' – the fleshier part at the back of the buttocks. This is sometimes done in self-preservation by certain riders, who have not yet learned to move with the horse. Rather than bump uncomfortably on the seat bones when in motion, many riders have a tendency to collapse the back and

The Fork Seat. This shows an unacceptable forward tilt of the pelvis and of the shoulders which places the weight of the rider almost entirely on her crotch. Unsupported by open buttocks and seatbones, the rider's back over-hollows and stiffens, so that the absorbing effect of the abdominal and loin muscles cannot take place. This leads to uncomfortable bouncing in the saddle.

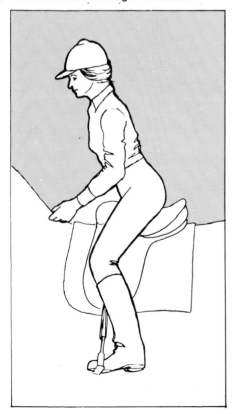

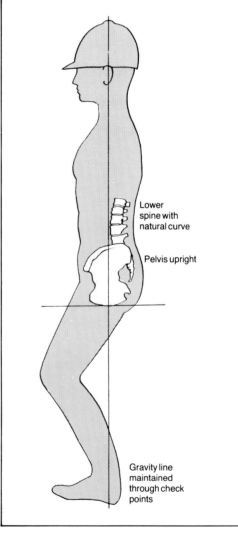

Lower spine with natural curve

Pelvis upright

Gravity line maintained through check points

BALANCED SEAT

tilt the pelvis backwards to such a degree that the seat bones come out of contact and rest their weight on the glutinous muscle at the back of their bottoms. This must be avoided at all cost. The expression 'tuck your tail in' is damaging to riders because invariably they do just that – and sit on the tail instead of the seat. (See below.)

What therefore should the super-slim rider do to remain comfortably on his seat bones? He will probably find the problem of discomfort disappears once he has learned to 'unlock' in the pelvic area and use his back. This is more a matter of suppling than anything else, but if the slightly bruised feeling persists, it is advisable in some cases to use a fluffy sheepskin covering over the saddle. This is far preferable to adopting an incorrect position.

On the other hand, there is the well-endowed rider who finds it difficult to sit deep due to layers of fatty tissue forming an obstruction between the saddle and the seat bones. Provided that the thigh

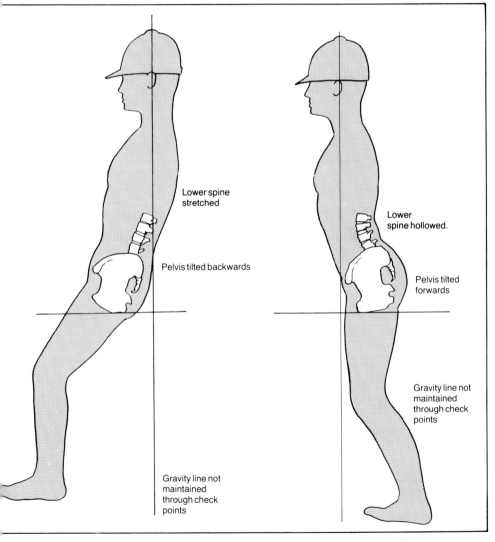

Lower spine stretched

Pelvis tilted backwards

Gravity line not maintained through check points

CHAIR SEAT

Lower spine hollowed.

Pelvis tilted forwards

Gravity line not maintained through check points

FORK SEAT

adjustment described previously is always made, as well as a very real conscious effort to open or spread the buttocks, this physical aspect should present little problem.

Having now established in one's mind where the points or surfaces of contact exist, and what it should feel like, and having made a conscious and physical effort to let nothing come between you and the saddle, there is a good chance of being able to remain comfortably in this position from now on. One last tip is to think of just your body with no legs attached having to balance in the saddle. Then everything we have described hitherto makes sense.

Confidence is gained when you realise the *whole seat* is in fullest contact with the saddle whilst still remaining upright and thus not losing balance. Providing we can maintain this security in motion we shall have achieved a truly independent Seat.

It is only when you are sitting there squarely, not assisted by the reins, but in balance supported by your own back, that you should put your limbs into the final position. And that is the easiest part of all, for having got the Seat absolutely right, the legs hang down naturally and find it easy to slip into a medium length stirrup. The arms too fall loosely and naturally into place with the elbows bent at the rider's side. Once the Seat is correct, central and deep everything else becomes second nature.

Now that we are sitting on the right part, in the right saddle and with the lessons of balance and self-carriage from the earlier chapters in our minds, we should by this time be looking elegant on our horse as he stands patiently waiting for an instruction to go forward.

MAINTAINING THE CLASSICAL SEAT IN MOTION

It is a testament to the sensitivity of the horse that despite the thick padding of sponge, leather and tree between his back and your Seat, not to mention all too often a fluffy numnah too, that he will know immediately when you ask him to go forward from the Seat. It is at this stage, that

the steadying effect we have achieved with the crotch is lightened or lifted. By easing the weight slightly backwards from our Basic Position, we engage the seat bones more deeply in the saddle. It is the seat bones together with the legs which now take up the main work of encouraging the horse forward and the feeling is one of pushing the waist towards the hands whilst remaining erect through the back and abdomen. This will result in a very much smoother transition than asking with the legs alone.

Once on the move, everyone has different ideas about the degree of tilt required in the pelvis to bring about the required Seat action for different movements. In the well-schooled horse, an upright, fairly neutral position is best at *all* times. From this Basic Position all we have to do is *ease the weight* in the required direction.

All too often however we see severe Seat aids being employed at all levels of competition. This is generally caused by a collapsing at the waist and a lack of support in the rider's back. Such movement often aggravates the horse's back and ruins any chance of achieving lightness and harmony. Small aids are always more effective than exaggerated commands and the best riders are those who appear to be constantly in the same upright, proud position.

At all times the rider should think in terms of balancing himself over the horse's centre of motion. Provided that this thought is constantly borne in mind, there should be little danger of abusing the horse with over-emphasised Seat aids. Remember too that the seat bones should be continually encouraging the horse *forwards*, and should never bear heavily downwards. This 'asking' with the Seat may be done in two ways.

1. Either by tightening the muscles in the lower back, thereby accentuating the natural curve of the loins into a more definite arch which advances the hip bone towards the hands. (Hence the expression 'push up to your hands'.)
Or:

2. By lengthening or stretching the loin muscles out of the natural curve so that the pelvis is rotated slightly backwards which brings the seat bones into a stronger contact with the saddle.

Both these small actions are brought about by the concertina muscles in the back working rather more actively than usual to allow the pelvis to rotate very slightly forwards or backwards. This action will manifest itself in the weight exerted on the various pressure points discussed by Handler in his description of the Seat aids. Again, it is only by feel that the sensitive rider will know how and when to employ this action. A little extra pressure on the seat bones (with the pelvis rotated slightly backwards) will invariably assist in lengthening the horse's stride provided that the rider is moving with the horse and merely accentuating the horse's own movement. The restraining influences of the front part of the Seat are also invaluable for precision work such as lateral

Too much thrust from the seat bones creates rider tension and stiffening in the horse's back.

movements and the collected gaits where the push forward of the seat bones may be applied laterally or together. These will be discussed in the last chapter.

There are infinite variations of the weight aids, but it is important between requests to return to a neutral position as a way of thanking the horse for his obedient response. The refined aids of the Seat should be invisible to the on-looker; apart from the rise and fall of his chest, the rider should look completely still in the saddle as the horse steps under his weight. Remember *all* the aids must work in harmony together.

FAULTS TO GUARD AGAINST

In cultivating the use of the Seat, we must guard against three serious faults:

1. The temptation to round the back and thrust crudely with the seat bones (often accompanied by a nodding head). This may look supple and impressive, but it is extremely unpleasant for the horse and unbalancing for the rider.

2. Stiffening the back by pulling in the stomach muscles and sitting only on the fork.

3. Setting up a movement of our own which is contrary to the motion of the horse. It is the horse which must at all times dictate our movement; only when, like good dancing partners, we are in tune with his movement, may we then emphasise and encourage him forward with our own sensitive Seat movement. **This should be so refined as to be invisible to the on-looker.**

Whilst some people liken the seat bones to a pair of rockers, the use of such a simile may encourage a swaying trunk. As we know, the trunk must remain as still as possible and I have found it much more helpful to think of my seat bones as two smoothing irons. Gently they smooth the material forward and iron out all the creases. The material represents my horse's back, and the creases are any tightness in his dorsal muscles. Once these are freed through subtle, encouraging massage, they will allow the horse greater performance with the hocks. The paradox of learning to move with your horse, which cannot be reiterated sufficiently, is that the on-looker should see you sitting very, very still. There is movement of course, but it is being taken up in the lower back, the stomach and round the ribcage where the 'concertina' (described earlier in the book) is softly playing. Once you have mastered this control, you and your horse will move as one.

In conclusion to the last three chapters, I feel it is a great pity that more is not taught about the use of the Seat. Whatever type of horse you ride there is no reason why you should not learn to move correctly with him in a soft, sympathetic way from the very beginning. As you progress together, you will learn how to refine your other aids and make riding so much easier for yourself. It is always a good idea however to have lessons on a more experienced horse so that you will always be learning the feel for the next stage with your own. On the advanced horse one reaches the stage where he becomes so light in hand and balanced beneath the saddle, that it is possible to move him forwards, sideways or backwards with the invisible Seat aids alone. But that of course is ultimate, and this stage of riding will not be reached until the rider has developed a heightened sense of that all-important ingredient – FEEL.

Strong but sensitive seats: Note in particular the braced back position of the horseman on the right as he accentuates the arch of the loins to obtain perfect lightness in hand.

The Legs
A BETTER UNDERSTANDING

Now that we have discussed in some depth the use of the Seat and the importance of a still, balanced trunk, both of which are governed by strong, flexible back muscles, we may now advance to examining in detail the function of the legs.

The effectiveness of the legs will be very much improved if the seat is well-established.

There is no doubt that despite the hours given over to the subject, tremendous confusion still exists in the minds of too many novice teachers and their pupils, not only about the correct leg position, but also the *function* of the legs. I can only think this is because no attention has been given to

the Seat in the first instance. When riding, it is a sad fact of life that if the pelvis is not correctly positioned, it is anatomically impossible to use the legs as God intended. Movements may become awkward and laboured if the bones of the leg are not correctly aligned in relation to the body.

MOBILITY AND FREEDOM OF THE LEG . . . ON THE GROUND

The biggest problem for the average rider which hampers the correct use of the leg is our old enemy – stiffness in the hip joint. Therefore again, much disappointment

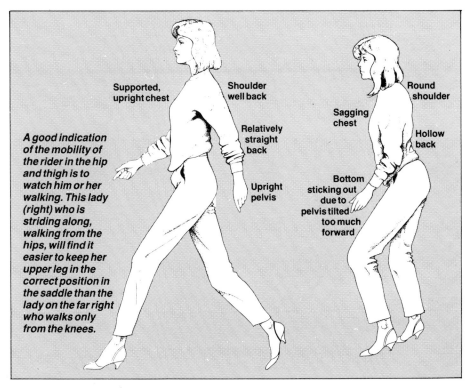

Supported, upright chest

Shoulder well back

Round shoulder

Sagging chest

Relatively straight back

Hollow back

A good indication of the mobility of the rider in the hip and thigh is to watch him or her walking. This lady (right) who is striding along, walking from the hips, will find it easier to keep her upper leg in the correct position in the saddle than the lady on the far right who walks only from the knees.

Upright pelvis

Bottom sticking out due to pelvis tilted too much forward

could be avoided if would-be dressage riders would only take practical steps on the ground to improve flexibility in this area. A good indication of the mobility of a rider in the hip and thigh is to watch him or her walking. The person who strides along, walking from the hips, i.e. with the pelvis upright and slightly in advance of the upper body to afford greater mobility to the legs, is normally more able to keep his/her upper leg in the correct position in the saddle than the person who walks only from the knees.

The latter type tends to run into trouble once mounted for reasons which are all too obvious. Whilst the poor lady illustrated (on page 41) may never have been aware of her failings during her meanderings on the ground, riding for her would be a struggle since she is clearly not in balance. Although riding is not a sport which requires block-busting physical strength, it does require athletic awareness and muscular control if it is to be carried out safely and efficiently. There is no doubt that

a general 'laziness' of the body will cause fatigue and an overall lack of energy in any event. One of the first areas to suffer is the rider's legs. Here the muscles are relatively large and will be quick to tire if made to work in a manner contrary to their natural function.

Looking on the brighter side, there is no doubt that people are becoming more posture-conscious. The amateur athlete, particularly those who jog, run, jump, ski, windsurf etc., will have excellent control of their legs from the hip, coupled with a keen sense of balance. People who work out of doors often move well; so do service men and women as a result of parade drill, and a model on a catwalk is normally a good example of someone who has to use her hips and thighs to full capacity. A supple, springy walk goes hand-in-hand with not only elegance but a general sense of purpose. Therefore if you really wish to achieve the maximum with your legs on the horse, start off by ensuring that you are truly mobile on the ground.

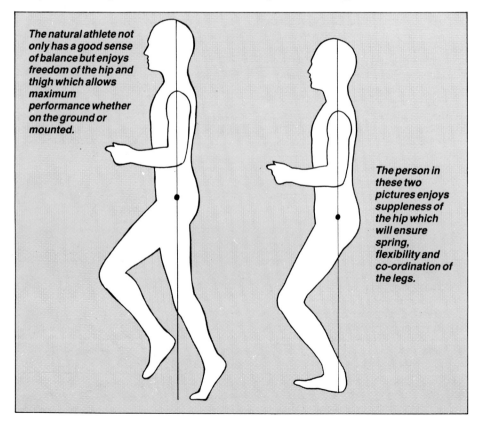

The natural athlete not only has a good sense of balance but enjoys freedom of the hip and thigh which allows maximum performance whether on the ground or mounted.

The person in these two pictures enjoys suppleness of the hip which will ensure spring, flexibility and co-ordination of the legs.

Surprisingly, probably the best exercise for learning to free the thighs is simply to improve your walk. Get a husband, boyfriend or father to encourage you to look more elegant if you are a girl. And men, don't be bashful, stop plodding and step out! By bringing the shoulders back, allowing the pelvis to come forward into an upright position, or tilted a little back, walk with a swing to your step, keeping the legs almost straight. Not only will you look better, but you will cover more ground with far less effort. Having increased your power of movement on the ground, it is time to put all this into practice on the horse.

. . . ON HORSEBACK

FIRSTLY. Remind yourself that the only difference in the position of the mounted figure and the unmounted figure is that in the former, the legs should be slightly bent at the knee. Therefore ease yourself quietly into the Basic Position and let your legs hang down, loose and free. To obtain total freedom of the leg, it is vital at this stage that you are aware of the full spread of the Seat as already described. Spreading the buttocks to form as broad a base underneath you as possible is very important as it will allow the leg to hang unconstricted away from the rider's body ready to embrace the barrel of the horse. With the horse standing still, make doubly sure of the pliancy of your joints and the independence of your legs by thinking about the horizontal section of the thigh (see page 34) and lifting the thigh outwards and away from the saddle. Do this first with one leg, then the other, and finally both legs. If your Seat is truly deep, you will not feel unbalanced by this exercise, and it will give you an idea of the mobility of the leg. After that you should feel supple enough and sufficiently in control of your limbs to tackle anything!

SECONDLY. Bring your leg quietly back into position. Carry out the thigh adjustment exercise which we described on page 34 and make sure that any flab is pulled away to the back of the femur. Now your thigh bone should be lying as close to the horse as possible. The inside of the male thigh is flatter in shape than the inside of the more rounded female thigh; so in theory a man ought to be able to lie his

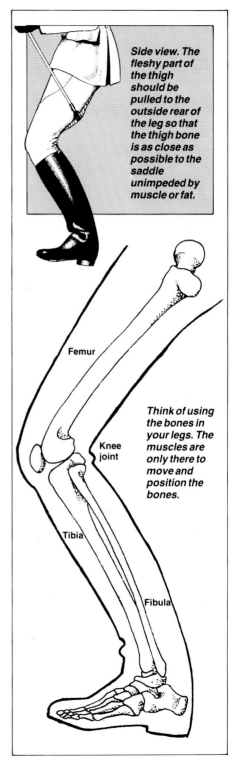

Side view. The fleshy part of the thigh should be pulled to the outside rear of the leg so that the thigh bone is as close as possible to the saddle unimpeded by muscle or fat.

Femur

Knee joint

Think of using the bones in your legs. The muscles are only there to move and position the bones.

Tibia

Fibula

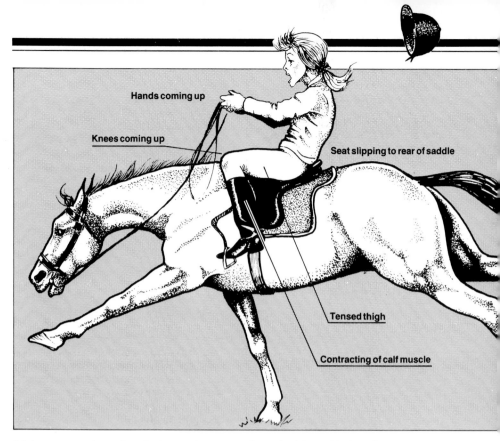

Hands coming up

Knees coming up

Seat slipping to rear of saddle

Tensed thigh

Contracting of calf muscle

thigh more snugly against the horse than a woman can.

It is a good idea when concentrating on the legs to think of using your leg bones rather than simply your leg muscles. After all, it is the all-embracing effect of your skeletal frame (i.e. the bones) rather than a mere tensing of muscle, which holds you into your saddle, and the legbones ultimately enable you to give the aids. Of course a very sensitive horse will feel the contracting, relaxing effect of the muscles particularly in the calf area, but do not lose sight of the fact that muscles exist to put the bones to work. This is what constitutes the aids, particularly in the leg. Once you begin to think in these terms, your leg aids will become positive and clearer. This will enable them to be short and easily transmitted to the horse. Prolonged squeezing and sustained pressure only leads to confusion and deadened sides. A short definite aid is easily understood and should produce a spontaneous result.

Simply bunching the leg muscles up underneath the bones does not only mislead the horse; in practice it tends to push the rider's frame *away* from the

horse's side and is therefore unseating as true contact is then lost.

I am sure we have all seen the unfortunate rider who, feeling him/herself lose balance in the saddle, tries to rectify the situation by gripping madly with the calf muscles. This inevitably brings the knee away from the saddle, and from thereon a snowball effect ensues. The thigh tenses and the rider loses his deep, snug contact with the thigh bone. This in turn causes the buttocks to tense causing the Seat to slide to the rear of the saddle. By this stage, the unbalanced horse only needs to drop a shoulder, give one small buck or sudden side-step and he has disposed of the encumbrance on his back! (See illustration.)

THIRDLY, and most importantly, it is imperative that the rider thinks of his leg in two separate parts with two quite different functions. (The degree of mental application required here is similar to that which we put into practice over 'separating' the upper body from the pelvis. Now we are seeking the same understanding of the mechanics of the leg.)

44

The reasons for dividing the leg into two different parts are as follows:

1. The upper leg or thigh works in conjunction with the Seat to keep the rider in place. It is therefore an integral part of the safety holding mechanism of the body, complemented by the independent Seat and the balancing effect of the trunk.

2. The lower leg is primarily used for the correct application of aids – again in conjunction with the aids of the Seat. It is not required for holding on.

Finally, the knee should be thought of as a continuation of the upper leg, but being a joint it must be flexible enough to give mobility to the lower leg which ought to be able to work in total freedom without disturbing the balance of the upper leg and Seat. Let us deal now specifically with –

THE UPPER LEG AND KNEE

At this stage it is helpful to have a picture of the pelvis and upper leg and knee in one integrated piece, soft, spread, supple and snug in the saddle. Provided that the Seat is correct, and the thigh allowed to settle as deeply downwards as comfortably possible, the entire contact area of these surfaces will become adhesive. There is no need to set up a vicelike grip with the thigh. The sheer weight of the thigh bone, unencumbered to the inside by fat or muscle will result in an extremely close contact with the saddle. In this position it is quite possible to maintain two pieces of paper between the thigh and the saddle flap in all gaits without actually trying very hard. There will be no need to grip and the rider should not tire, for the muscles are being required to do little. All that the rider has done is to put himself into the best position where gravity and balance may work through him. His earlier lessons in attaining feel on the lunge and an understanding of the deep central seat will by now have served him very well.

How deep should the thigh be in the saddle? Basically, the depth of the thigh in the saddle and the angle it makes with the lower leg is determined by the length of the stirrup. The knee should at all times be as low as the stirrup allows, and we have already seen the effects of the Chair Seat through a heightened knee (i.e. buttocks to the rear of the saddle, etc.,) – something which we have been avoiding throughout these chapters. It is obvious therefore that the stirrup should not be finally adjusted until the rider is happy with his Seat and able to determine just how low he can comfortably keep his knee whilst still maintaining his stirrup. Provided that he follows the maxim of the perpendicular line through the approximate checkpoints of the ear, point of shoulder, hip joint and anklebone, it is more than likely that the knee will be sufficiently low. This will automatically allow the thigh to be sufficiently deep.

Only by keeping the knee and the thigh fairly low may the rider exert true influence on the whole leg for the purpose of accurate work on the flat.

Returning to the theme of safety which must at all times prevail, a popular cliché used to a worrying degree nowadays by indifferent instructors is: "Take the knee away from the saddle!" More dangerous advice could hardly be given to the inexperienced rider. It is an unfortunate sign of the times that many an expression such as this is heard on the lips of a truly great instructor and then gets passed

Some riders go through their equestrian life with their leg constantly in this position. Note the gripping calf has pulled the heel upward and caused a tense thigh. Such a leg will in time deaden the horse's side.

down the line to end up with a young, inexperienced assistant instructor teaching a class of novices. What is forgotten on the way is that the expression was probably originally used for a specific reason at a particular stage of training for advanced riders on their advanced horses.

In the context of assisting such pupils to accomplish correct leg aids for lateral or elevated work where greater freedom of the lower leg is required, taking the knee very slightly away from the saddle can be advantageous. Applied as a general rule however, particularly with the inexperienced, such a command is courting a fall and possibly a nasty accident.

HOW TO USE THE UPPER LEG AND KNEE

If you study the human frame (i.e. the bones) it is, again, commonsense that shows what should or should not be done. By moving the knee joint outwards, we are losing the close, natural contact our thigh has made against the horse. This will allow the outer, fleshy part of the thigh to turn inwards and the leg is rotated away from the saddle. From thereon the leg will have to grip hard if it is to remain in contact, and with the increased tension the deep, balanced Seat will be lost. The heel will also be affected and drawn upwards.

Before progressing to explore the uses of the lower leg, it would be wise to discuss the occasion when you may wish to employ knee and thigh grip as opposed to the more natural close contact approach. Although this book is concerned with work on the flat, it should be mentioned here that there is nothing against a more conscious grip when riding cross-country and when you wish to take the weight off the horse's back in order to gallop and allow him more freedom and impulsion. This would obviously follow for race riding and to a certain extent for jumping. I prefer to think about taking my weight on my knees rather than gripping hard with the knee to avoid muscle tension. There is no doubt however that turning the knee deeply inwards gives the upper leg a pretty vice-like clamp, which is infinitely preferable to keeping oneself up and forward with the reins. The clamp-like action of the thighs is also invaluable in any sort of emergency and the more oblique the angle of the leg, the stronger it becomes.

Having confirmed then that the main task of the upper leg in riding is to maintain a close contact with the horse and help to hold the rider in place, I would add at this stage that a very highly schooled horse will actually recognise aids from the thigh bones for impulsion, even though these aids are normally given by the lower leg. One does not wish to confuse readers by continually pointing out exceptions to the rule, but if one did not allow that they existed, this would not allow for the unexpected. Riding therefore must never become so regimented that under certain circumstances, a change of emphasis is precluded. Whilst riding is a very practical science, it must be remembered that it is also, thankfully, an art. The true artist will know when some special action is required, and he will be sufficiently disciplined to sense when a particular horse requires a different approach. Thus the very sensitive horse may be able to dispense with the lower leg aids and will show the rider that all he requires is a closer contact with the thigh bones and aids directed solely through weight. Such awareness comes only after years of practice and discovery.

There is one other area where thigh aids would be preferable to those of the lower leg, and this would be in the case of a very long-legged rider riding a horse which is not well-ribbed up. If the lower leg is hanging so far down beneath the horse's girth that it is awkward to apply an aid, then the horse must be taught to listen more to the thigh and the seat aids.

However, neither of the above set of circumstances should affect the average rider too greatly, and our rule of thumb as originally set out, is:

Upper leg works with the seat to keep you in place.

Lower leg works independently of the upper leg for the correct application of the aids.

47

The Legs
OUR WORKING AIDS

In the last chapter we noted;
The lower leg is primarily used for the correct application of aids – in conjunction with the Seat aids. It is not required for holding on.

CONTROL OF THE LOWER LEG

Ideally, the novice rider should not be taught the use of the lower leg until, on the lunge, he is able without stirrups to keep his knee and thigh low and close, and the lower leg relaxed and long. If the rider has the inclination to grip up with the lower leg the moment the horse begins to move forward it will be obvious to the instructor that his Seat is not yet independent.

With the more experienced rider, it does no harm to remind oneself of the independence of the lower leg by carrying out a simple exercise. With the horse in walk, and keeping your knee against the saddle (without grip) try to swing your lower leg outwards a little and then backwards and forwards freely without touching the horse's side. This will ensure suppleness of the knee joint and conscious control of the lower leg.

Now return your foot to the stirrup and take up the normal leg position. Your leg should be lightly against your horse's side. Ensure that your foot is lying roughly parallel to the horse's side although a very slight turn outwards may be necessary to keep your leg just in contact. (This depends on how well ribbed-up your horse is.) Be careful however that in seeking this contact the calf muscles do not begin to grip and bunch up under the lower leg. As with the thigh, we are seeking a contact with the inside of the leg in readiness for the giving of aids. At this stage it is only sensible to remind ourselves why we must not hold onto the horse with the lower leg. There are several reasons:

1. Holding on with the lower leg or calf brings the knee away from the saddle and this in turn causes the thigh to reduce contact.

2. Sustained pressure on the horse's side with the lower leg is the signal to go forward. Therefore if one is continually pressing the horse forward, when he is already going actively forward, he should theoretically be permanently in gallop! What happens in practice is that being confused by this permanent instruction from the calf, the horse will tend to ignore it and eventually his sides become dead to the leg.

3. If you allow yourself to grow into the habit of gripping witn the lower leg to stabilise yourself, once you change to a sensitive schooled horse, you risk trouble. Gripping in this way activates his 'accelerator button' and he may leap forward causing you to lose balance. Thus such a practice can be dangerous.

4. By gripping with the lower leg you no longer leave it free to apply the aids. Sadly this happens all too often and the rider has to resort to the use of heels, spurs and whip to achieve a response.

THE IDEAL POSITION

Whilst the position of the thigh and knee is determined largely by the length of stirrup, the position of the lower leg may be adjusted forward or back at will. It is important however that it is correctly aligned within the framework of our perpendicular line. If not it may spoil all that we have achieved so far. Of course, only you will know what is absolutely right for your own comfort, safety and performance when it comes to the exact position of the leg, and a few centimetres on either side of our plumbline need not be disastrous. However try to aim for the ideal, for apart from safety, the giving of aids is so much simpler if the general guidelines are followed. What is the easiest way of keeping the lower leg somewhere around the ideal area?

There is no doubt at all that if we get the

A long, low, relaxed knee will allow the rider to settle down comfortably into the centre of the saddle. Once this can be maintained in motion, it will be obvious the rider has achieved a good, independent seat.

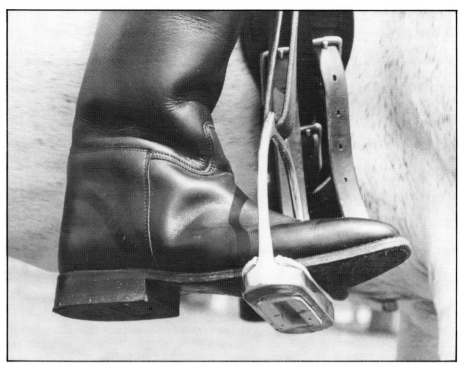

foot correct in the stirrup, we have a good chance of maintaining a correct lower leg position. Let us therefore examine the foot position before discussing the aids and their application.

Again, a logical approach is necessary. It stands to reason that provided there is minimal muscle tension, i.e. all the weight is going down from the knee into the lower leg and towards the ground (weight must go down as per the law of gravity) it is going to earth itself into the foot – being the lowest part of the body. For the sake of keeping our stirrups from slipping off and because also it is important to keep this weight back rather than forward, the natural outlet for this weight is in the heel. Understanding this allows the rider to drop the heel from an unconstricted leg, rather than pushing down forcefully as is so often employed by beginners when they are told "Push down with your heels!" Pushing too strongly will only tense the leg and in fact may reduce the weight into the buttocks.

The stirrup, as we all know, should rest on the ball of the foot. The easiest way to keep it there is to incline the foot very slightly towards the horse's side. By this I do not mean turn the toes inwards – the

It is often easier to keep the ball of the foot in the stirrup by allowing the inside of the foot to be a little lower than the outside.

toes should at all times be looking roughly forward – what is suggested is that we relax our ankles and allow the inside of the foot to be a little lower than the outside. In this position, anybody looking at us from the side should just be able to see the outer sole of the boot (see photo).

This very slight incline from a soft ankle will help to hold the stirrup firmly in one position and at the same time has the effect of keeping our knee close to the saddle. It is the safest form of holding the stirrup, for pressing hard against the stirrup with the ball of the foot will tend to slide the lower leg forward and the buttocks to the rear of the saddle.

Talking to a well-known cavalry instructor recently, I was interested to hear that in his day teaching raw recruits of the Household Cavalry, many of whom had never had a formal riding lesson in their life, the simplest way of achieving a correct leg position was to concentrate only on the foot. By arranging the foot in the manner described above, the leg was never

50

mentioned until a much later stage.

Another tip to maintain the stirrup without tensing and pushing down, is to think of it as nothing more than a comfortable foot rest. We have already noted in this book time and time again how mental images help to produce the required result in riding without force, and this is a good example. A foot rest – somewhere to place your foot and relieve it of its own weight and be comfortable. Provided that we remember that stirrups are normally lost because of tension in the lower leg muscles which bring the foot up an inch or so with every stride, we should be able to soften the lower leg and keep the stirrup in the right place with little ado.

PREPARING FOR THE LEG AIDS

At last, having achieved a good basic position with the whole leg, we have reached the stage where the giving of aids to the horse may be conducted, naturally, correctly and comfortably.
What in short are the main aids?

1. The lower leg acting just behind the girth asks the horse to bring his hindlegs further underneath to make him go forward with energy. This is known as creating impulsion.

2. The lower leg acting two or three inches further back asks the horse to step sideways. This is brought about by the fact that with applied pressure on the inside seat bone the horse tries to step under the centre of gravity of the rider to maintain his own balance.

As well as activating, the lower leg also supports, directs, limits, controls, encourages, allows and makes possible every variation of turn and of forward, lateral, backward, and, in *haute ecole,* even upward work of the horse in all the gaits.

Before discussing how, when and more exactly where we apply these aids, let us consider carefully the true meaning of this word.

Most equestrian books will tell you an 'aid' is a signal or an instruction to the horse. The simple Oxford Dictionary meaning is usually by-passed; yet the first explanation which is offered for the verb 'to aid' is 'to help'. The appropriate suggestion

for the noun is 'anything helpful'. With this in mind, we discover that by applying push or a nudge with our lower leg on certain pressure points of the horse's side, we are actually helping him to carry out what we want. The leg aids can therefore be very much more than mere signals.

One of the first things we teach the horse after his initial basic training, is to move away from the leg when pressure is applied on one side or the other. The horse steps obediently sideways, but all he is really doing is recovering his balance by stepping underneath our centre of gravity. We have literally *helped* him to achieve an obedient response.

Equitation, with its basic mechanical laws has been probed and studied for literally thousands of years. What has been handed down to us in the form of simple aids is a legacy of accumulated knowledge. Therefore the practice of 'button pressing' with the lower leg is not so much the issuing of a command; rather, it is a matter of the rider putting the horse into a position where he is helped to go in the direction required without losing balance.

The late Colonel Podhajsky, former director of the Spanish Riding School, has this to say on the subject with regard to the lateral aids when the outside leg is applying the appropriate aid: "When the weight of the body is transferred into the direction of the lateral movement, it will support the effect of the outside leg because the horse will try to step under the centre of gravity of the rider."

It is important that we realise every time we apply an aid and the horse responds, the pressure must then be eased. This is the only way in which we may indicate to the horse that he has obeyed us. *The alleviation of the aid is his reward.* Of course to maintain a good, balanced gait, it may be necessary to re-apply the aid for impulsion with every stride, although the intensity of the aid should not be as strong as it was in the initial instance. As the horse begins to understand what you want, you may eventually be able to keep everything going smoothly forward with your Seat alone. Trial and error through feel is the only way to find out, but never forget that it is as important to tell the horse that he has got it right, as it is to ask him to do it in the first place.

A DISCERNING APPLICATION OF THE AIDS

All through this book I have avoided where possible the use of fashionable equestrian clichés which may mislead the reader. 'Pushing the right button' is indeed a catch phrase, but provided we know which button to press, this does sum up a helpful picture which should enable us to be more discerning with our leg aids.

Unfortunately it is not always sufficiently explained where 'the right button' lies on the horse's side and many riders are extremely vague as to where they should apply pressure for different movements. "Legs on!" is a command which resounds several times a day round the walls of most riding schools, yet few instructors will take the trouble to explain exactly which part of the horse's anatomy the legs must be 'on'.

For accurate riding, therefore, it is a good idea to picture a panel of buttons on the horse's side. Careful use and respect for these will help us to become true artists on horseback. The area over which these imaginery buttons are spread is small. As the horse becomes better schooled and more responsive to the leg, this area will decrease until happily there will come a time when only one button need be employed. This stage is reached when the horse becomes so attuned to the nuances of your seat and of the weight aids which are activated every time you press a button with your lower leg, that he will respond to the lightest touch on the smallest possible area. This of course takes time and patience.

Now study the pressure points on our 'panel' in more detail. Remember that:

1. Not necessarily will our legs be acting together on the same buttons at the same time. The right leg may press Button A while the left leg is engaged on Button B. The children's co-ordination test of patting the head and rubbing the tummy is similar to the type of co-ordination required by the rider when he wishes for example to execute a turn on the hocks to the right. His right leg will be steadying the horse at the forehand, and applying just enough impulsion to prevent the horse stepping backwards; his left leg will be acting quite strongly in a steady squeeze requesting the turn around the inside leg. Two quite

different leg aids, in two different positions, performed simultaneously.

2. In the words of Podhajsky: "The effect of the legs must become more and more refined in the course of training. With a green horse this aid will at first be a short and distinct action of the lower leg . . . The pressure of the rider's legs must be decreased the moment the horse has responded to his demands."

With all this in mind, we may now examine the various buttons in detail until an understanding of their uses becomes second nature. For many natural riders, this feel comes automatically through their acute sense of balance; for others it may be helpful to have this simple guide.

BUTTON A – Probably our most important button. The whole area around this spot and upwards towards the *top of the rider's boot is included in this pressure spot and it is first and foremost our **Impulsion Button.** Situated at the girth or just behind it, pressure here with the foot and lower leg will assist the horse to move his hindlegs further underneath him. Therefore he is able to go forward more efficiently and actively. In basic terms, it acts as an accelerator. Don't forget however, as soon as a response is felt, the rider must ease the aid just as he/she would when driving a car. If you keep your foot permanently on the accelerator when out driving at the original firm pressure, you would not now be sitting down to read this book!

Button A (or a little forward) is also the propitious area in which to apply an aid for **supporting the forehand** in a turn on the haunches or in a half-pass; for bending the horse round the inside leg (so that he bends evenly throughout his body from head to tail) yet keeping the impulsion forward during shoulder-in. It is also the button for initiating and maintaining the canter and is applied at the girth on the same side as the lead foreleg.

BUTTON B and the whole area around and above (again to almost the *top of the boot) is the pressure point to indicate to the horse that you do not wish his quarters to stray outwards (very useful if hacking along a narrow path by a ditch for example). Used with stronger, more sustained pressure (until the horse

---

* This depends very much on the length of the riders's leg.

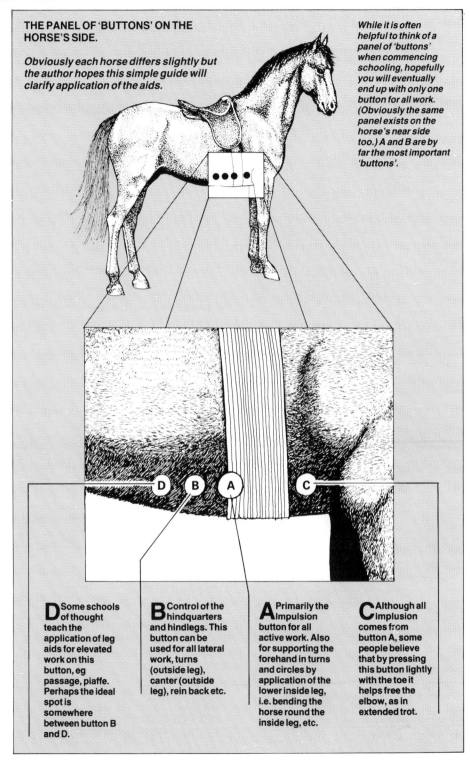

THE PANEL OF 'BUTTONS' ON THE HORSE'S SIDE.

Obviously each horse differs slightly but the author hopes this simple guide will clarify application of the aids.

While it is often helpful to think of a panel of 'buttons' when commencing schooling, hopefully you will eventually end up with only one button for all work. (Obviously the same panel exists on the horse's near side too.) A and B are by far the most important 'buttons'.

D Some schools of thought teach the application of leg aids for elevated work on this button, eg passage, piaffe. Perhaps the ideal spot is somewhere between button B and D.

B Control of the hindquarters and hindlegs. This button can be used for all lateral work, turns (outside leg), canter (outside leg), rein back etc.

A Primarily the Impulsion button for all active work. Also for supporting the forehand in turns and circles by application of the lower inside leg, i.e. bending the horse round the inside leg, etc.

C Although all impulsion comes from button A, some people believe that by pressing this button lightly with the toe it helps free the elbow, as in extended trot.

In the shoulder-in the inside leg maintains the bend and aids impulsion whilst the outside leg controls and directs the hindquarters. As in the photograph these aids should be subtle yet positive.

responds) this aid has the effect of actually making the horse step away from the leg. This would be appropriate in both the turns (on the forehand and on the hock), half-pass, leg-yield, etc. Together with the Seat aids, a stronger leg aid at this point asks the horse in fact to *move away from the leg*. (Note that a 'stronger' leg aid does not imply a kick.)

Button B is also the pressure point to indicate to the hindleg of the same side that you wish to canter. The canter gait is a series of bounds and the first complete bound forward comes from the opposite hindleg of the leading foreleg. An excellent exercise to improve your feel for the canter is to try cantering yourself on the ground. You will see that your leading leg cannot leap forward unless you push yourself off with the opposite leg. Although the horse has four legs and you only have two, the principle remains the same. Therefore your outside leg at Button B will help to activate the horse's outside hind (but don't forget also to ask with your inside leg at Button A as described overleaf).

In canter to the right, the sequence is: left hind, the diagonal pair (i.e. right hind and left fore) and *finally* the inside leading right fore.

In rein-back, we normally apply pressure with both legs somewhere between Button A and Button B. They create the impulsion, whilst the Seat initiates the movement back. The legs then control the quarters and prevent them from swinging outwards in order to achieve a straight rein-back.

BUTTON C may be correctly used to encourage the horse to go freely forward from the shoulder provided that the correct degree of impulsion has been obtained from Button A. Never fall into the error of thinking that Button C will give impulsion. But once the required impulsion is already there, then, by using the toe in a light press or squeeze again Button C, you may find your horse will respond by stretching forward more with a freer elbow. Such an aid is particularly useful when teaching the horse to extend in the trot, or to lengthen the walk – but again the leg must return to its normal place when the horse responds to this aid.

BUTTON D should only be used for achieving a high degree of collection and for elevated work where the horse is being encouraged to bring his hocks as far underneath him as possible and to raise his forehand. (See photo below.) There are many schools of thought as to the exact location of the 'collection button'. Great instructors speak of the lower leg stretching downwards towards the horse's hind feet and this invariably implies a position well back. From my own experience I have found the most effective activating spot to be roughly as illustrated, although others will disagree. Probably photographs showing great riders working their horses in the various highly collected exercises – such as the one illustrated – are more helpful than anything as one can pinpoint the leg position for each exercise.

It is important to realise that the employment of Button D is not for the everyday rider and there is nothing less attractive or more unkind than seeing heels or spurs being applied on or behind this area. By making people more aware of the special use of this 'button', hopefully, any abuse by the lower leg here will be avoided.

As with the Seat aids, readers should constantly remind themselves that the application of a leg aid carried out without feel is worthless. All the aids must work together and the leg aids must be combined with corresponding assistance for the Seat, back and hands. It is a waste of time to push, say, Button A for forward impulsion if you are blocking the movement in your horse's back by sitting down hard on your fork, with your shoulders

forward, and your hands like clay. A sensitive horse would probably respond to such an aid by shooting straight backwards!

Also never forget that a unilateral aid must be accompanied by a supportive aid on the other side. A good rule is to say to yourself before applying any positive leg aid: "What should my other leg be doing and where?"

Finally never forget that each horse is different. In Charles Harris's excellent book *Fundamentals of Riding* (J. A. Allen & Co.) the action of the lower leg and heel applied singly or together is described. They may "press, caress, stroke, pinch, nudge, strike or kick". The first three actions are obviously far preferable and there is no reason at all why the horse should not accept these stimulii – particularly in the case of a young horse. With the older horse, should his sides feel somewhat wooden, start off with a light aid, and then gradually strengthen each attempt until he responds. Then make much of him. The time will come when he will listen to the light aids, and the stronger aid will become a thing of the past.

One last thought – La Guerinière always spoke of 'a breathing leg'. Xenophon spoke of a supple leg which could yield, "without at all disturbing the thigh." Allow your legs to feel, to 'breathe' and to mould themselves to the horse and be very, very clear in your head as to their two quite separate yet equally important functions.

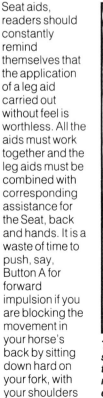

To obtain a high degree of collection or elevation, some riders will draw the lower leg well back behind the girth to apply the aid; others, such as the great master illustrated above, are able to achieve the same effect without an exaggerated leg aid.

The Hands
REINS OF SILK

"Anything forced or misunderstood can never be beautiful . . ."

The above sentiment applies as much today as it did in the time of Xenophon, and in particular perhaps to that much misunderstood subject, the hands.

It is no accident of fate that I have left the chapters on the hands to the end of this book. The rein influence on the horse comes only *after one has put him to the aids of the back, the Seat and the legs.*

THE RELATIONSHIP BETWEEN HANDS AND SEAT

We hear a great deal nowadays about the horse being 'between hand and leg'. I find this expression limited and all too reminiscent of the fact that so little is taught about that essential ingredient, the Seat. I do not personally believe the rider can develop a really good hand with the leg aids alone. If we study the great masters of classical equitation we will note that the stillest, kindest hands prevail where the rider sits deep so that the buttocks are spread to form the broad base of support we have discussed at such length, and the chest is upright and proud. In this way the rider is able to control the horse's muscles through his 'top line' into the hand, as well as activating his legs. It is important to be aware of this before discussing the use of the hands.

The hands are the fine instruments which talk to the horse and through the action of the bit maintain a polite conversation, telling him in which direction we wish him to go and in what manner. The hands constitute the finishing touches to the picture – harmoniously channelling all the energy which our body and leg aids have created. One does not need a Grand Prix dressage horse to ride elegantly and correctly. It is perfectly possible to strive towards attaining a classical seat with excellent hands on a perfectly ordinary riding school horse. With gentle persuasion, a positive feel for the subject and the application of correct aids, a nose-poking plodder can be transformed into a horse of presence before the eyes. Provided that there is nothing physically wrong with the horse, there should be no such word as 'can't'!

HOW TO USE THE HANDS

Not so long ago, you were not considered a good horseman or horsewoman unless you were born with light, tactful hands. Good hands were the essence of good horsemanship and the highest compliment a serious rider could receive was the remark – "he has wonderful hands". It went without saying of course that the person concerned would also have a good seat which included all that went with it – control, balance, energy and harmony. Such riders can work miracles with the most obstinate of horses.

Today, in the average riding lesson, less and less emphasis appears to be placed on how the hands are *used*. Instructors will take great pains to establish the position of the rider's hand in front of the saddle, but it is rare that one hears an explanation of how that position may be maintained with the hands gentle yet effective.

"Keep the hands light!" "Talk to the horse through your fingers!" "Play with the reins!" Expressions such as these are helpful and immediately conjure up the need for artistry. Sadly nowadays it only seems to be the country's top trainers – most of whom have trained abroad – who use them. In the average lesson the current emphasis is on establishing a contact. There is nothing wrong with this in itself, but the manner in which this may be, and often is, interpreted is frequently crude.

At lower levels of teaching, one may observe too many examples of riders with a 'good contact' to be none other than a cluster of people with fixed, unyielding

Only a light hand will bring about true harmony between horse and rider, as exemplified eight times over above.

hands hauling their horses' heads into an artificial position – the idea being that they have achieved a good 'outline'. So much for fashion. This story might be laughable if it were not for the fact that it happens time and time again all over the country and is often practised in the name of scholarship with the apparent approval of the instructors concerned.

It is fairly obvious that this state of affairs exists because too little attention has been paid to the rider's Seat in the first instance. It is possible also that much of this can be blamed on the attitude which exists concerning the snaffle bit.

The snaffle is an excellent bit but it was originally designed for flat racing, or for use by grooms who were deemed to be of insufficient education to be let loose with a 'proper bit'. The 'proper bit' was, of course, the double bridle, the prerogative of the horse's owner. Times have changed;

The line from the rider's elbow through the forearm, wrist and hand to the horse's mouth should be unbroken (as above) although at a more advanced stage the hand will be held higher.

A weak seat invariably leads to harsh, punitive hands, especially in times of trouble (see above). Note how this has come about through tense, gripping calves, raised knee, loss of contact with thigh and fork, and the seat slipping to rear of saddle.

riding has become largely do-it-yourself; gone are the days when every horse was *schooled* before he was passed on to the prospective purchaser. Nowadays, the double bridle is looked upon as something rather special or remedial, either just for dressage or showing or for horses with a hard mouth. The snaffle is now the accepted bit of the day and one is constantly exhorted as to its mildness. This has lulled many riders into a false sense of security and they truly believe that they can do no harm with a 'mere' snaffle. On the contrary, you have to be a very good rider with a great degree of tact to get the best use from the snaffle.

If you are doubtful about your hands, and your horse does not seem happy in the mouth, it could be you are using the wrong snaffle. In hands which tend to see-saw for

example, a thin, jointed, ringed snaffle could turn out to be an instrument of torture. It is better by far to play safe and go always for the thick snaffle on an eggbutt, or a snaffle with cheeks. If you really want a mild bit, the half-moon and straight-bar unjointed snaffle is excellent particularly for a horse whose mouth is very sensitive. And please, however many times you may have seen it on television, or in the collecting ring before a dressage competition – never *ever* allow your hands to see-saw on the reins.

Although not strictly classical, with certain pupils on certain horses I have often found the vulcanite or rubber pelham a kinder bit. The two reins (without couplings) have the effect of making the rider *think* about his hands, instead of allowing them to hang on the rein, like two dead weights.

It is a pity that pupils are not made more aware of the pitfalls of bad hands. It is not uncommon to find a bleeding mouth in the hunting field and even in top-level dressage competitions we observe some unpleasant sights, largely caused by punitively busy hands. Those riders who do use their hands artistically are sadly not always rewarded for their sensitivity and may pass without credit. The system of marking still takes little account of the quality of riding although many people would like to see this changed. Insufficient attention is therefore paid both at grassroots and at public eye level to artistry; the result is too many horses with unhappy mouths and often a natural resistance to dressage from the general public.

CONTACT – THE LINK BETWEEN THE RIDER'S HANDS AND THE HORSE'S MOUTH

Much nonsense, as we have seen, is talked about 'contact'. Contact is quite simply the link between the rider's hands and the mouth of the horse. There is nothing complex or marvellous about it. A simple requirement, it should be light and positive. In the well-schooled horse, the weight of the reins alone can bring about sufficient contact. In the young horse the contact will be stronger, although never more than two or three ounces and the contact is then maintained by pushing the horse up to the hand with the Seat, back and legs. If more was talked about lightness instead of 'contact', I am convinced we would have better riders with better hands.

Contact should never take the form of long, sustained pulls on the reins. If this happens, the horse will lean on the bit and become heavy on his forehand. As the horse is much stronger than the rider, the horse invariably wins in a pulling match. That great French horseman of the last century, François Baucher, said: "Never pull on your reins and you will always have pleasant, manageable horses that are easy to ride."

It is unfortunately true that pulling hands make for pulling horses. Because people are not always prepared nowadays to spend the necessary hours to develop a good seat from which will come good hands, all manner of artificial gadgets are produced. Some of the more unyielding nosebands are particularly bad since they deny the horse any freedom in the lower jaw. A horse must have freedom if he is to flex and soften; therefore many of these gadgets are self-destructive.

Even with a difficult horse, there is simply no need for any rider to pull or be heavy-handed if he accepts the basic classical ground rules which have been reiterated in this book. The horse cannot pull against the rider who has a firm base of support.

With the horse which tries to take hold, the rider must firmly resist a pulling match. Meet resistance with resistance by pushing up to your hands from a strong Seat. To assist your balance and the firmness of your Seat, you may wish to bring your shoulders back a little behind the perpendicular line, but be very careful not to collapse your back. Now close your fingers tightly on the rein and work hard with your legs. Push the horse determinedly forward into your hand. Provided that you do not allow the slightest divergence of your elbows from the perpendicular line, the horse will quickly learn from this not to pull against himself. The best thing about this effective but subtle course of action is that at no time will you have to pull on the horse's mouth. Your fingers may remain gentle and your hand light throughout; yet *you* will be in control.

To establish a good contact therefore, we should ride from a strong position into a light hand. We all tend to do too much with our hands and not enough with our backs, Seat and legs. Get into the habit of thinking of the hands last. Make them quiet. Once you have achieved quietness and lightness you will be well on the way towards attaining a happy, obedient and responsive horse.

The effect of a light, asking hand should never be underestimated. To help achieve that lightness, here are two approaches to consider before you ride:

1. Allow the horse to feel the elasticity of your elbow and never the weight of your hands.

2. Think of your hands as fine precision instruments, rather like the delicate,

It is perfectly possible to maintain the horse in balance on the lightest of contacts as this line drawing of François Baucher demonstrates.

refined implements a surgeon uses throughout an intricate operation. Every tiny movement made by your fingers will be felt; every turn, every slight of hand will make all the difference between success or failure. Be ultra-discerning, like the surgeon!

Before we go on to discuss in more detail the role and exact position of the shoulder, the arm, the wrist and the hand, we would do well to remind ourselves of an old Spanish proverb . . . "To ride is to aspire to gentleness. Ride with reins of silk!"

The Hands
OUR PRECISION AIDS

As the use of the hands is governed so delicately by the rider's sense of feel, it would be misleading to write too extensively on the different nuances of movement and control which can be achieved. Once you have explained to a child what the paintbrush and paints are for and provided him with paper, he has to develop the technique of painting for himself. He may be guided, shown what not to do, helped by example, but the act of painting and the result which manifests itself on the paper is, in the end, his and his alone. It is the same in riding. To ride really well you must first have a picture of what good riding is, and by keeping the classical principles in mind, you should know and feel when the picture is right and good.

The main rule is to keep everything as simple as possible. Try to stay within the framework of the perpendicular line and allow your body weight to be absorbed by you and the horse – never to escape

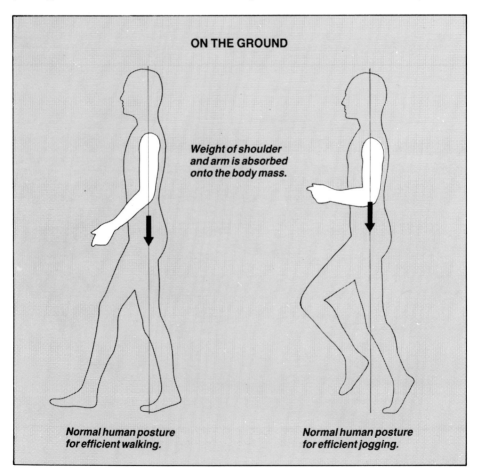

ON THE GROUND

Weight of shoulder and arm is absorbed onto the body mass.

Normal human posture for efficient walking.

Normal human posture for efficient jogging.

through your hands into the reins.

Studiously avoid contortions with your hands which do not ascribe to the two correct positions on page 67. Always copy the great masters and do not be hoodwinked into trying artificial positions simply because they are the latest vogue at horse shows. A few pictures from the Spanish Riding School or Saumur scattered around the tackroom is no bad thing. You will *never* see incorrect positions of the shoulder, elbow, arm or hand – and it makes no difference if the rider is mounted on a young or advanced horse.

Let us now, point by point, examine the overall picture:

SHOULDERS

Starting at the top, we know that the shoulders should be open and back. It is very important that they are not allowed to slouch forward, for they form the fixed point in our gravity line and by bringing them forward, balance will be lost.

There are a number of occasions however when they may be brought slightly *behind* the gravity line as we have already seen and these will be discussed further in the next chapter.

Remember that the head and shoulder brought forward of the gravitational line will render the Seat virtually ineffectual and the rider will become a passenger; whereas the shoulder well back will give an effective Seat.

In an attempt to sit up straight, be careful that you do not raise your shoulders. Always think of the weight of the shoulder flowing downwards, i.e. from the point of shoulder into the elbow, from the elbow into the hip. It is fashionable in riding lessons to

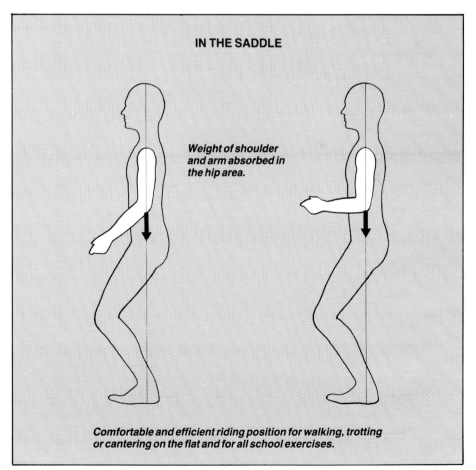

IN THE SADDLE

Weight of shoulder and arm absorbed in the hip area.

Comfortable and efficient riding position for walking, trotting or cantering on the flat and for all school exercises.

be told to imagine that a string or a wire is pulling the head upwards and out of the shoulders. This is excellent but in 'growing tall' guard against stiffening the neck and raising the shoulders and then forgetting to bring them down again. This will restrict the use of the rider's back and seat and cause stiffness in the upper arm.

UPPER ARM

Once the shoulders are correct, the upper arm will hang down easily and unconstrained within the perpendicular line, neither gripping the sides of the body nor coming too far outwards. The upper arm is well endowed with muscles, and it is comforting to know that in the event of a possible struggle with a pulling horse, the upper arm may become steel-like, whilst the hands still remain light and gentle.

Generally speaking however, the upper arm should be relaxed enough to hang down naturally, yet sufficiently supported to carry the forearm lightly. This has the effect of bringing the elbows within the gravity line as already discussed.

ELBOWS

There is nothing complicated about the ideal way to carry the elbows in the classical riding position. Think, as ever, about what you would do on the ground when walking or jogging and the answer is plain to see. You do not have to be a riding expert to appreciate that if for the majority of work the shoulders and elbows are kept within the direct body line, there is no reason for the forearm, wrist and hand to be heavy. The joints in the elbow are elastic and will be at their most efficient if the

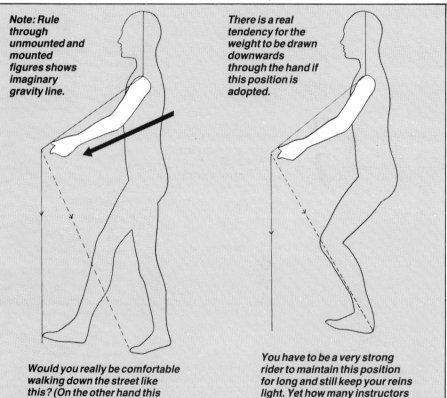

Note: Rule through unmounted and mounted figures shows imaginary gravity line.

There is a real tendency for the weight to be drawn downwards through the hand if this position is adopted.

Would you really be comfortable walking down the street like this? (On the other hand this fixed arm position is ideal for pushing a supermarket trolley where you require some driving force in your hands.)

You have to be a very strong rider to maintain this position for long and still keep your reins light. Yet how many instructors start off novice pupils by pulling their elbows away from their sides? Don't we make things difficult for ourselves?

elbow is contained within the body line. At the same time, the body will absorb the entire weight of the shoulder and upper arm *provided* that the elbow is not brought out of alignment. Once, however, we move the elbow out and away from the trunk, there is always the danger of weight being directed into the hand. *It takes a very real concentrated effort to keep the hands light once the elbow is no longer contained within the body framework.*

At the same time take care not to grip with the elbows into the sides. Elbows pressed firmly against the body will again lose their elasticity and mar the downward weight flow from the shoulders and upper arm. Too far out, they will break the natural line, i.e. elbow to wrist to hand, if the hands are to remain reasonably close on either side of the horse's neck. Too far back, they will cause the hands to be too close to the

rider's body and true control of the rein will be lost. With the elbows correctly and comfortably in position, it is not difficult to keep the hands light and still.

There are of course occasions when you may wish to bring the elbows out of alignment, but do not get into the habit of keeping them there, otherwise your horse will find it difficult to come off his forehand.

There are a number of exercises with problem horses where it may be necessary to bring the whole arm forward in order to encourage the horse to build up the correct muscles in his neck. In walk on a long rein for example in a dressage test, or at the

A horse will tend to go on his forehand when the rider brings the elbow in front of the perpendicular body line. In this photo, the weight of the rider's shoulders is being carried into the hand, causing stiffness in both horse and rider.

end of work we may of course bring the elbows forward slightly to allow the horse to stretch forward and down, but much nonsense is talked about bringing the elbows severely forward for extended movements. This is of no benefit to the horse who is quite able to lengthen with the arm in the normal classical position. (See photo on page 70.)

A correct position of the elbow is not always given sufficient emphasis in riding lessons. It is the elbow which absorbs the movements which the horse makes with his head. To allow the elbow to give and ease, the thumbs must be carried uppermost, otherwise the joint becomes less flexible. Never pull back with the elbows. If the rein is the correct length, a very slight easing of the forearm up or down from the elbow together with the play of the fingers will allow the hands to act quietly and positively.

Even with the young horse working in a longer, lower outline at walk, it is possible to sit classically. Note in particular the classical arm position. (Photo reproduced by kind permission of Eva Podhajsky.)

FOREARM, WRIST AND HAND

At all times think of stillness and quietness in the wrists and hands. The forearms carry the hands which should form a straight but supple line to the horse's mouth, unbroken at the wrists. The movements carried out by the forearms may be up and down but this should never be sudden (and never more than approximately 15 degrees or so from the parallel) or equally correctly they may be sideways or turning (rotational). They must never ever pull back.

With the more advanced horse, the rider generally keeps his forearm parallel to the ground – roughly in line with his waist. With the novice horse, he may prefer to lower the forearm so that his little finger is resting just above the pommel of the saddle. The expression *descente de main* is a way of thanking the horse and easing the rein for a movement well done, or a relaxation of the lower jaw. It may either constitute an actual lowering of the hand, or it may merely be a relaxation of the fingers, which the balanced horse will automatically feel.

Do not let the wrists sag. There must be

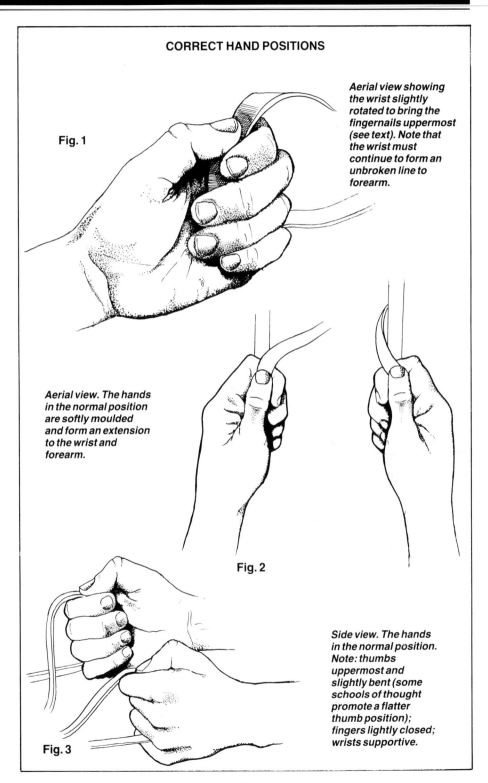

CORRECT HAND POSITIONS

Fig. 1

Aerial view showing the wrist slightly rotated to bring the fingernails uppermost (see text). Note that the wrist must continue to form an unbroken line to forearm.

Aerial view. The hands in the normal position are softly moulded and form an extension to the wrist and forearm.

Fig. 2

Side view. The hands in the normal position. Note: thumbs uppermost and slightly bent (some schools of thought promote a flatter thumb position); fingers lightly closed; wrists supportive.

Fig. 3

INCORRECT HAND POSITIONS

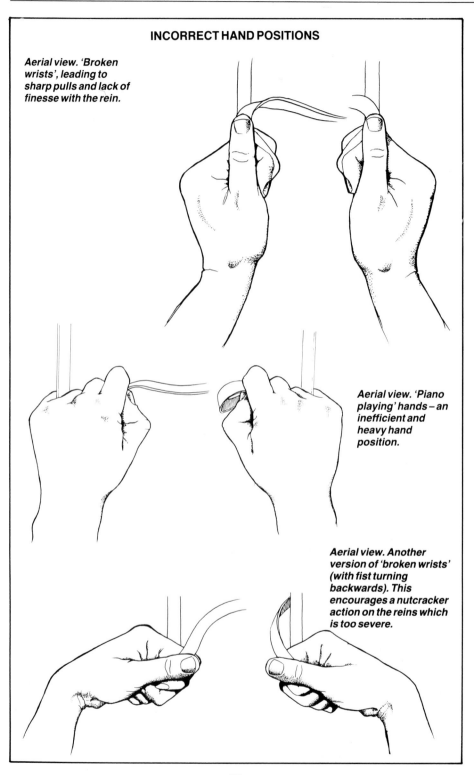

Aerial view. 'Broken wrists', leading to sharp pulls and lack of finesse with the rein.

Aerial view. 'Piano playing' hands – an inefficient and heavy hand position.

Aerial view. Another version of 'broken wrists' (with fist turning backwards). This encourages a nutcracker action on the reins which is too severe.

sufficient support in the wrists to keep the hands light. The wrist should be an extension to the forearm, therefore if you turn your wrist you actually turn your forearm too. In keeping the wrist and forearm supportive, do guard against rigidity. In the same way that a rigid Seat causes the rider to bump around in the saddle, a rigid forearm may cause the hands to jab the horse in the mouth. The paradox of good riding, as we have already noted, is that by allowing the horse to move you and absorbing that movement in a series of quiet, counter movements, i.e. with the back, pelvis and finally the elbows, forearms, wrists and hands, you eventually achieve a semblance of great stillness. Naturally, all these counter movements should be so miniscule that they are invisible to the onlooker.

From now on, we shall examine the two fundamental positions of the hands (see diagram on page 67). The hands should remain on either side of the horse's neck and at no time should one rein cross over the neck to the side of the other. They may also support at the neck if required.

BASIC POSITION

Figures 2 and 3 show the hands in the normal position where a straight line is maintained with the forearm, where the thumb is uppermost and slightly bent to secure the rein, and the fingers are lightly closed to direct the rein. Do not tightly clench the fingers when you wish to ride forward. It is the thumb which prevents the rein from slipping and a certain mobility in the fingers is most desirable. A sensitive horse will respond to a little vibrato played on the rein by the third and fourth finger as this helps to relax his jaw, encouraging him to chew gently so that the flow of saliva keeps his mouth soft and the bit lubricated. With the reins held lightly in this way with a slightly 'open' finger, extra pressure (taking up one to two inches of rein) can be applied at a moment's notice simply by clenching the fingers as required. When both hands are used, this squeezing of the fingers should be quite sufficient to check, to change the gait, or to bring the horse to halt. When one hand is used, it should be sufficient to turn the horse in the same direction. This hand, brought very slightly

forward and outward, becomes the 'opening hand'. This effective action with the fingers is known as 'asking' or 'taking', and the rein can be relaxed again swiftly by simply opening the fingers slightly and 'giving' the moment the horse obeys.

ROTATED POSITION

By rotating the wrist, a position much advocated by La Guerinière and the Classical School, the hands may be brought into the position illustrated in Figure 1 which shows the fingernails beginning to face upwards. This has the effect also of gently shortening the rein and is used for all exercises where the hand wishes to invite the horse into a turn, a circle, or a lateral movement. By bringing the hand slightly forward and rotating the wrist in this way, this hand requests the horse to follow the direction of the rein. Thus the horse may be quietly led off the track into whatever movement the rider wishes to make, e.g. with the right hand, into right shoulder-in; with the left hand, into left half-pass, etc.

Obviously, such a rein aid must be applied in conjunction with the Seat, back and leg aids, but the well-schooled horse will respond readily to this slight turn of the wrist bringing the fingers uppermost. The supporting rein on the outside may also be slightly rotated for extra precision and is equally important to dictate the degree of bend.

With the correct rein contact and a feeling for the above two positions which will come quite naturally provided that you grill yourself into never pulling backwards, every possible movement may be achieved with quiet hands.

Never allow yourself to fall into the horrible practice of bringing your hand back towards the hip or, worse, behind the hip in order to turn your horse. Neither should your hand move outwards from the withers to the extent that the bit begins to be pulled through the horse's mouth as is all too often seen.

Practise instead the *small* aids of the hands. Keep your hands just in front of the pommel, roughly three to four inches apart and get into the habit of:

a) playing with your fingers in order to give and take with the rein so that the horse learns to respect your hand and to act upon it, i.e. to flex, to go forward, lengthen, increase the energy etc., or to check, slow down, halt.

b) rotating your wrist and turning your fingers uppermost so that the horse recognises the request with one hand to turn, step sideways or change direction, etc; or to steady, half-halt, halt or rein back when both hands are used.

So often pupils have wailed: "It's all very well teaching such refined aids with schooled horses but what about me and my young, newly backed four-year-old?" Inexperience or youth in a horse is simply no excuse for resorting to crude aids. It just means you have to work harder to get the message through. As Podhajsky says: "If, with a young horse, the first action with the reins does not lead to success, the reins should yield and the action be repeated until success is obtained." Certainly at the onset of training, the rider may find he has to employ the whole arm more positively in his control of the rein, but the upper arm,

elbow, forearm, wrist and fingers should still never diverge more than an inch or so from the basic classical position. As Podhajsky goes on: "To be able to give the aids simply by turning the hands is the ultimate aim of training and can be achieved only by long and systematic work."

Nothing is easy, but if we start as we mean to go on, we will get there. A happy horse whose rider has good hands will enjoy his bit and there will be a continual feedback from him as he carries it proudly and lightly. There is no greater joy than a horse with whom we can communicate in this way; that reward makes every inch of the work along the way worthwhile.

A perfect position! Even in this extravagant extended trot, Colonel Podhajsky maintains the bent elbow, forearms parallel to the ground, supportive wrist and light hand. A fine example of classical riding at its best which every pupil at every level should be encouraged to attain. (Photo reproduced by kind permission of Eva Podhajsky.)

Riding forward with confidence

A whole new way of riding awaits the rider who has successfully grasped the basics of the all-embracing Classical Seat both on the lunge and off it, with and without stirrups.

The object of good riding, as we have been anxious to point out throughout this book, is to maintain that independent Seat at every gait so that we may have maximum control with our legs and employ the lightest of hands at all times. In order to help the reader accomplish this, we have at times risked becoming repetitive about the importance of the Seat and back. Time and again the importance of cultivating depth and balance through an upright pelvis and a supportive, erect trunk has been stressed. However, all the hours spent assimilating these facts and putting them into practice will never be wasted. The reward will be the opening of many a door, previously closed, and the sure conviction that you may now go on learning for the rest of your life.

So often I have heard the words, "I seem to have gone as far as I can. I feel I've reached the end of the road with my riding. I've no idea where to go from here." Such words are the hallmark of a person who has never experienced the feeling of a deep Classical Seat. Without that sensation of control, it is hardly surprising that they feel they can go no further. The shallow Seat which they may well have been taught from early childhood to be the correct one and which may have afforded them a modicum of success at lower levels has finally imprisoned them with its limitations. Once they have reached a certain stage of riding and schooling, they can indeed go no further. How tragic to be taught bad habits at the beginning! It is always harder to relearn the right way, than to start off correctly from day one. Consolation however can be derived – as I know from my own experience – from being more able to help and understand others. Those who have learned and transformed a weak Seat into a balanced Seat, will be sympathetic of the problems.

It may be that, having come to the last chapter of this book, the reader will be discouraged from trying to aim for the stars by the fact that he or she has not yet experienced a canter pirouette, a perfect flying change or even really knows what it feels like to achieve a good collected walk. If you have never experienced these sensations how can you ever aim for them? You may well ask.

It is very much easier to improve one's position if you are first able to experiment on a kind, patient yet athletic schoolmaster. The strong-backed Warm-Bloods and the Irish Draught, Welsh Cob crosses are often excellent schoolmasters. Many of the great riding academies of the world go one step further and employ the short-coupled Lipizzaner, Lusitano and Andalusian horse for this very purpose, i.e. to give pupils the feel of balance and movements correctly done. These particular breeds not only have superb, unflappable temperaments, they also have short, wide loins which give them the suppleness required to engage their hocks deeply underneath them and raise the forehand with ease. For a pupil who has only ridden horses which trundle along on their forehands, such a sensation of fingertip authority comes as a revelation.

Do not be discouraged when you first return to the horse you usually ride after lessons on a good schoolmaster. The feelings you have achieved with the schoolmaster will stay within you and you will have a very vivid idea of what is required for the future with your own horse. Storing up a *library of feelings* is the essence of learning to ride well; when you get a good feeling, mentally file it and store it away. Then, when you are trying to attain a particular movement with your own horse, recall that file and remind yourself of the feeling – just like delving into a reference book in a library. This is known as riding with your mind as well as your body. Your 'library of feelings' will help you to balance your horse and to know when you have got it right. In time all these wonderful feelings will become part of everyday life with your own horse.

Many people are put off dressage by what they regard to be grandiose terms. The various dressage movements are not nearly as formidable as they sound and are within reach once you have trained yourself to sit correctly and to balance the horse through your Seat. It is not the purpose of this book however to guide the reader through all the aids for each and every manoeuvre. There are already many excellent books which will help you to achieve these as and when you feel ready to progress to each stage.

In this final chapter however, we are concerned with some lasting thoughts and ideas, based on all that we have discussed so far. In recapitulation therefore, here are some helpful observations to guide you on the path of riding forward with confidence and towards feeling what is happening underneath you.

This will improve your sense of balance and give the horse confidence. Horses have an uncanny knack of sensing when you look down. This has been proved time and time again when riding over jumps. The rider who looks far ahead and over the jump will enjoy success after success; the rider whose gaze stops at the rail is nine times out of ten inviting a refusal. Many a good dressage test is spoiled by the rider clenching his jaw, sticking his chin out and bringing the whole head out of alignment. This will encourage a stiff neck, taut shoulders and ultimately a heavy hand. Horses whose riders cannot carry their heads lightly and in alignment usually have trouble coming off their forehands. Therefore look up, and look forward.

Remember that if the shoulders are brought too much in advance of the perpendicular line, the Seat will be rendered virtually ineffectual. Remember also that riders invariably fall off forwards; rarely backwards.

Therefore in your flatwork always keep the shoulders open and back. In times of trouble, bringing the shoulders actually *behind* the perpendicular line whilst keeping your hips pressed forward will strengthen the Seat. There are many occasions when such action is helpful:

1. If the horse is trying to pull against your hands, you will be able to overcome his resistance by your own resistance, i.e. by bringing your shoulders back and pushing more strongly forward from the seat bones against him. In this way, a runaway horse with a hard mouth may be brought under control, whereas pulling on the reins from an insecure seat will achieve little.

2. If you are riding a lazy horse who will not respond to the leg aids to go forward, it is often very helpful to bring the shoulders back and again push on strongly with more Seat.

3. If the horse is shying at or evading some object, a slight shift in weight by bringing the shoulders back will again make for a more effective Seat and assist the legs in encouraging him past the obstacle.

4. When asking your horse to extend in walk, trot or canter, you may find it helpful to bring your shoulders a little more back than usual to enable more push from the seat bones. *In other words, the above examples serve to demonstrate how the*

There are certain occasions when bringing the shoulders actually behind the perpendicular line whilst keeping the hips pressed forward will strengthen the Seat – but what a pity the rider is looking down!

position of the shoulders affects the stability and strength of the Seat but this will only work if the back is kept supported and the hips well forward.

Remember the importance of a full, open, expanded chest.

Not only will this assist your breathing but it will help to keep your back supported and encourage an upright pelvis. Thus the breathing mechanism of the muscles around your ribcage and pelvis will be able to operate in freedom. Picture the proudest rider you know and note the fullness of his chest.

Remind yourself of the shock absorber effect of the muscles in the lower back.

If you try to stretch the lower back *too* much, you will lose the elasticity of the loins. Be conscious always of the three point seat even when your weight is largely on the two seat bones. When bringing the shoulders back, guard against tilting the

whole trunk backwards, thus stretching the loins and making the Seat rigid.

As we have seen, the best way to become truly familiar with the influences of the Seat and the feel of the seat bones working together or separately is to practise on the lunge. The best results are achieved without stirrups on a blanket held in place with a vaulting saddle. But you can equally practise this in a normal saddle when hacking quietly along a lane. Relax the buttocks, allow the horse to move you and become aware of which seat bone is coming forward at which moment. Once you have developed a feeling for what is happening at each gait, you will be in a position to encourage or to accentuate that movement by merely applying rather more pressure on the seat bones at the relevant moment. This push forward may be

applied as follows:

1. In the walk, the right seat bone will move forward very slightly in advance of the left one, as the horse steps under his body with his right hind. In the same way, the left seat bone advances slightly in front of the other, as the left hindhoof comes down. The quality and length of the gait may be emphasised by the rider slightly accentuating the pressure on each seat bone as *alternately* they are moved forward.

Perfect collection. Suddenly we have absolute authority at our finger-tips even with one hand! How much safer we would be if our horses were soft and collected like this for more of the time.

2. In the trot however, the feeling is very different. Here the seat bones work together as the concertina muscles in the small of the back absorb the up and down sensation derived through the pelvis as each diagonal pair of legs hits the ground. *Together,* the seat bones may encourage a

lengthened stride by pushing rather more strongly with the shoulders well back; or, by bringing the pelvis more upright and using the restraining influences of the Seat, collection may be obtained. This is described in more detail further on.

3. In canter the feeling in the seat bones is dictated by the horse's leading leg. If the horse is cantering with his right or off-fore leading, the right side of the horse's body will be carried a little in advance of the left. Therefore the rider's weight should be directed rather more into the right seatbone than the left and this is more easily achieved by deepening the knee on the right side which can only be achieved from a light, flexible ankle. Beware however of collapsing the right hip and allowing the seat to slide to the outside of the saddle. It is as important in the canter as it is in the more bouncy trot, to keep the trunk well supported. As the canter is a series of bounds, the legs should at all times initiate and encourage each bound whilst the driving forward or restraining influence of the Seat dictates the length and the impulsion of the stride.

4. For work on the circle, there will always be a little more weight directed into the inner seat bone. This will be the same for turns when the rider's weight directed through the seat bone of the same side invites the horse to turn with him, i.e. turn to the right, weight into right seat bone. Turn to the left, weight into left seat bone.

5. In lateral work, the seat bones again play an active role. The inner seat bone should be weighted in shoulder-in, half-pass, renvers, travers, and so on but as with the canter, guard against the tendency to collapse the inside hip and allow your seat to slip to the outside. This will often happen if the inside leg, in attempting to stretch down, is not sufficiently forward on the girth. It must give the horse something to bend around.

It will also produce tension in the buttocks which causes the Seat to bounce in the saddle. Allow the tummy muscles to soften; then grow tall from the waist to support the spine.

Think of your legs as flexible, working assets to assist, encourage, and control your horse. Remember that they are also the vehicles via which much of your weight is carried downwards through the imaginary gravity line, and as such must not become muscle-bound and restricted. Allow your legs to maintain a never-ending dialogue of instructions to the horse's 'engine'. In short, use your legs but with a positive idea of what you want them to do.

SAFETY

Never ever forget that you owe it to yourself and your horse to be safe in the saddle. Except for the lucky few, gone are the days when it was something of a joke if you fell off out hacking. Someone would be bound to catch your horse and you could all have a good drink in the pub later to console yourself and thank the obliging fellow who had caught your runaway mount.

Nowadays, things have changed. Firstly, huge, hungry motorways sever the countryside. Secondly, little country lanes, once the haunt of the local squire and his farm workers, swarm with fast commuter cars all speeding to the city. There are less pedestrians about, and certainly fewer capable of catching a frightened bolting horse. The horrifying number of accidents involving horses whose riders have been thrown, mounts by the week. So often these horses are horribly maimed if not killed outright and have to be destroyed. As for riding, statistics show it is now considered to be the most dangerous sport in Great Britain today with the highest number of fatal accidents. The answer to this whole problem is all too painfully clear:

1. Riders must be taught methods which will give them as much security and control as possible.

2. All road users should honour the Highway Code's ruling regarding horses and become aware of the necessity whenever possible to slow down for horses and to give them a wide.berth.

3. Correctly fitting and secured hats

which match up to the BSI standard should be worn at all times.

Official equestrian bodies and the leading equestrian magazines are taking positive steps to deal with the second and third question. It would seem that not enough is being done about the first. A preoccupation with 'what is good for the horse' has often taken precedence over proper safety procedures for the rider, and this of course ends up being *not at all good for the horse*.

For example, sitting deeply into the saddle is often discouraged in case it 'harms the horse's back'; and a child which quite clearly cannot control its pony in a snaffle bit is discouraged from using a double bridle or a pelham to the detriment of their combined safety. Whilst the latter may not be ideal, at least the priorities are there. We may draw comfort from the fact however that it *is* possible to sit in such a way that maximum control can be achieved. One of the ways in which this may be done is to teach riders more about collection.

COLLECTION

People still talk about collection as though it were an artificial state produced solely for the dressage arena. It is often forgotten that horses in their own natural environment very often collect themselves – particularly when showing off in front of other horses when they wish to be in a state of readiness for whatever action is required.

In simple terms, collection may be considered as keeping the horse on the bit in a state of controlled and active balance, so that he becomes immediately obedient to the aids in all the gaits. From the collected state, he can be turned, reined-back, made to side-step, or go forward with great impulsion, all without hesitation. Consider by contrast the horse who is allowed always to proceed along on his forehand. Simply because he is not together, it is going to take very much longer to achieve a response to the aids. In adverse circumstances, this horse can actually be a liability, as well as being far less pleasurable to ride.

Recently, in a well-known international equestrian magazine, an interesting article on collection appeared by Clemens Dierks, formerly a Bereiter at the Warendorf Centre in Germany. Now teaching dressage and schooling to Grand Prix level in Australia he had this to say about the average horse and rider in his newly adopted continent. "When I came to this country and I rode horses, everybody told me how light they were. When I picked up the reins, they either completely rejected that and reared in the air or they were fighting for their head. They had always been ridden on a loose rein, which automatically gives people a light feeling in their hands. The horses were never truly on the bit and engaged from behind. They were not in self-carriage, they were just going on the forehand."

This is all too true of the average person who hacks his horse out on the roads, lanes and tracks of Britain today. No wonder there are so many accidents! With a shallow seat, and the horse permanently on his forehand, very little can be done quickly in an emergency.

How therefore may we achieve collection?

One of the most precious influences of the deep, classical Seat is its ability to assist in collection and extension. If you are truly able to sit in the manner described in these pages, to feel and absorb the movement of the horse, you are in a position to school your horse towards collection. There is no reason why the horse should not start learning the basics of collection once his basic training is established. In a healthy, fit horse this can be done at around the age of five.

Collection, correctly done, is not a restricting state for the horse; rather it should give the horse more scope. Never confuse collection with the floating, dainty steps we have come to see in some show hacks and ponies. The animal which arches its neck, tucks its chin in, rounds its outline and prettily points its toes may well be fooling us. If it is not tracking up well behind and flexing in all three joints of the hindleg, it will not be in true collection. Collection must be accompanied by impulsion – the difference is, it will be *contained* impulsion. This will only come with great sensitivity from a strong Seat with the patient application of the aids which we have already described. At the

beginning it is best practised at the walk until you are sure you are getting the results you want.

We have already seen how extension is obtained by bringing the shoulders a little behind the vertical line and pushing more strongly forwards with the seat bones assisted by the impulsion giving aids of the legs. Collection is altogether a different feeling. Here again the seat bones must work together, but from a more upright position. Once the rider's weight is well forward the horse is able to soften the back and lighten the forehand unhampered by the rider's Seat. It is at this stage of riding that a feeling for the three point seat becomes so vitally important.

The collecting influences of the rider's Seat come via the muscles of the lower back. Tightening these increases the arch of the loins. This eases the weight slightly onto the crotch and inside thighs which

Sympathetic hands invite the horse into the pirouette whilst the rider's seat and leg aids regulate the movement. Thus the horse's energy is guided upward, resulting in a light forehand with the hocks well-engaged.

helps to direct the horse's energy upwards, rounded and forwards, rather than low, flat and forwards. These aids will only be effective if at all times the legs produce sufficient impulsion for the Seat to channel its flow. By playing softly on the reins with light, asking fingers, the horse will relax in the jaw and begin to flex from the poll. Gradually the rider will find he has concentrated all that wonderful energy into a rounder horse and a more athletic horse. Suddenly, the horse is totally under him, part of him, and he has fingertip control.

Many of us have never experienced any other feeling from an energetic horse except that he is continually running away in front of us. He may not necessarily pull, but there is always that inescapable sensation that he is out there in front with his long neck, and we are literally being taken for a ride. The uninitiated believe that the only way to control the front is to haul it in, shorten it and then give directives. How much more comfortable and safer the rider would be if he could school his horse forward into collection.

Once in collection there is no question of the horse being on his forehand or out of control. Suddenly, we have absolute authority, yet are able to administer it in the gentlest way possible. What has actually happened is that without losing impulsion, the horse has shortened and concentrated his gait so that it becomes more elevated. With the hocks now coming more deeply underneath the body mass, the forehand is controllable. From now on the rider can request the horse to move in any direction he wishes, and the horse will respond. Not five seconds later, not a second later, but straightaway – as the thought enters our head! In balance, which is a truly wonderful sensation, not to be abused.

If you are fortunate enough to be offered collection from your horse for the first time – make do in the beginning with a few strides. Then reward him by relaxing the muscles in the lower back, easing the leg aids, giving a little more with the rein and allowing the horse to flow forwards into a longer outline again. Make much of him with hand and voice and he will remember how clever he has been. Once he has this assurance, he will be happier and happier about offering you collection until it becomes part of his working day, not just something for the dressage arena, but for normal riding out. From now on, you will be a safer rider.

The other day, I received a surprise visit from a charming middle-aged lady who had come as a pupil to my late husband and myself some six years before at our Dressage School in Suffolk. She had brought her own horse, then a somewhat green, rather wilful six-year-old Thoroughbred cross Connemara mare. After six days of morning lunge lessons on a blanket without stirrups, followed by two hours on our advanced horses, and then an hour on her own horse, enormous progress had been made. She left our

establishment full of intentions to return, but life's events overtook us both and I never saw her again. That was – not until this summer.

I was delighted to hear from her that she still had her little mare, and that she still rode daily. She had never gone in for dressage competitions she said, because she got so much pleasure from just improving her horse quietly on her own and doing the odd hunter trial. "You know you saved my life," she said out of the blue as we were reminiscing about all the schoolwork she had undergone during her course six years before. I looked at her incredulously and wondered what was coming. "What do you mean?"

"Oh yes," she said with quiet firmness. "Just the other day in fact, Sparrow and I were trotting down a quiet but very narrow country lane near my home in Kent, when round the corner came two enormous juggernauts, one behind the other. They were bearing down so fast I realised they would never be able to brake in time. The first was coming straight at me. There was nowhere to escape to except a very tiny strip of grass at the edge of the road. There was no room to turn and certainly not enough time. There was only one thing to do and I just prayed it would work. I put my leg against Sparrow and immediately she stepped neatly to the side. A perfect response. If her quarters had swung out, we would have been killed. Those lorries passed us both within a whisker."

I felt very moved that this nice lady should have given us any credit whatsoever. We had never got as far as half-pass or shoulder-in with Sparrow but we had worked on collection and leg-yielding and once her owner had started to sit classically she had begun to discover the tremendous influence of the leg over a not particularly amenable little mare.

Therefore, whether you, like Sparrow's owner, just want to enjoy your riding more and gain a deeper, more positive control of both yourself and the horse you ride, or whether you want to reach for the stars and represent your country in competition, perhaps doesn't really matter very much.

What matters is holding the key to the future. Once you find that the key not only fits the lock but opens the door, riding will never be the same again.